Meditations on Angels

Coloring Book

Series 1

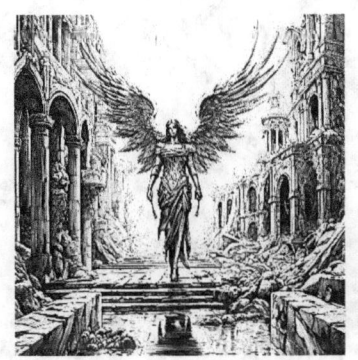

Josephine Christiansen © 2023

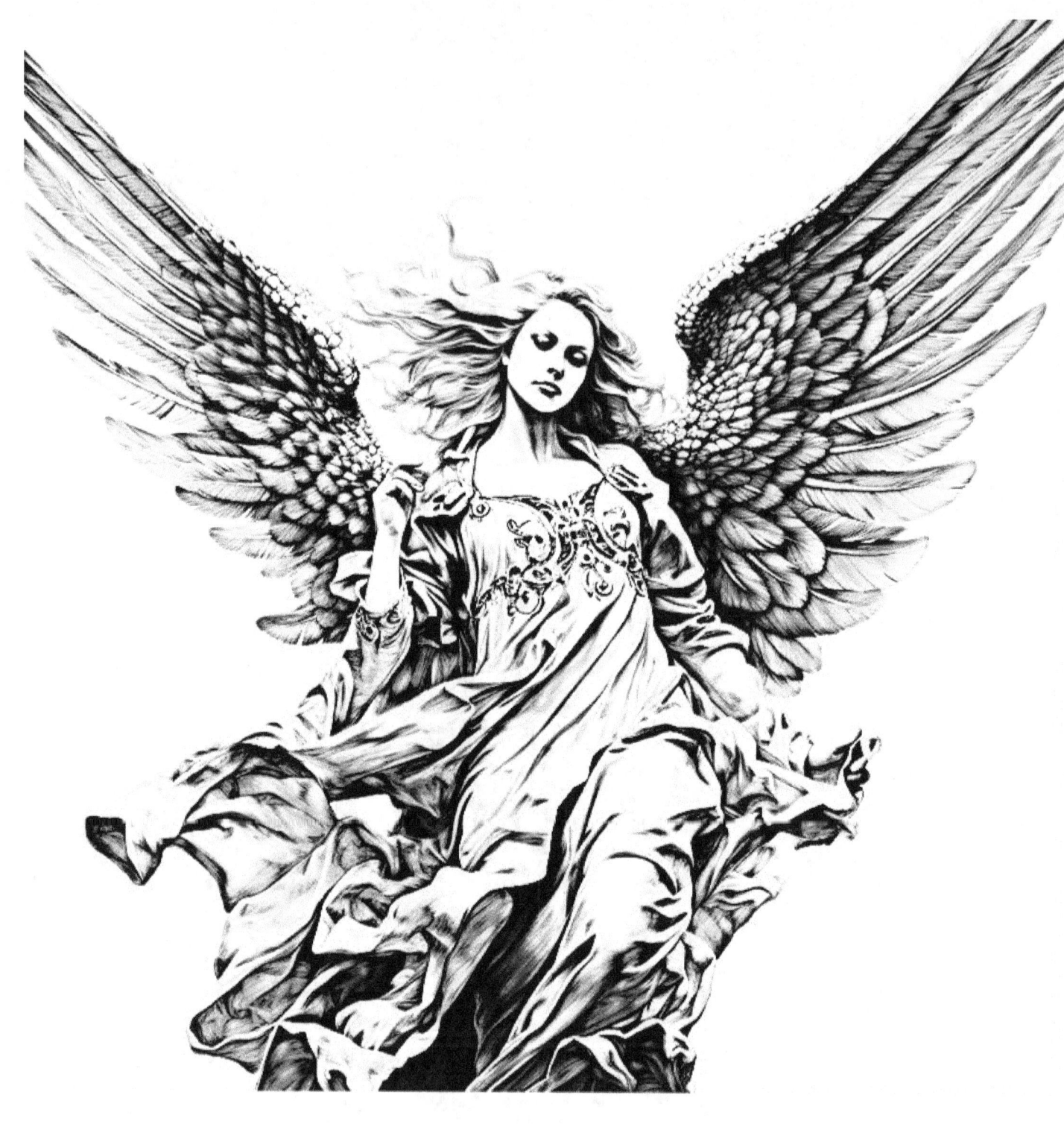

1 Corinthians 4:9

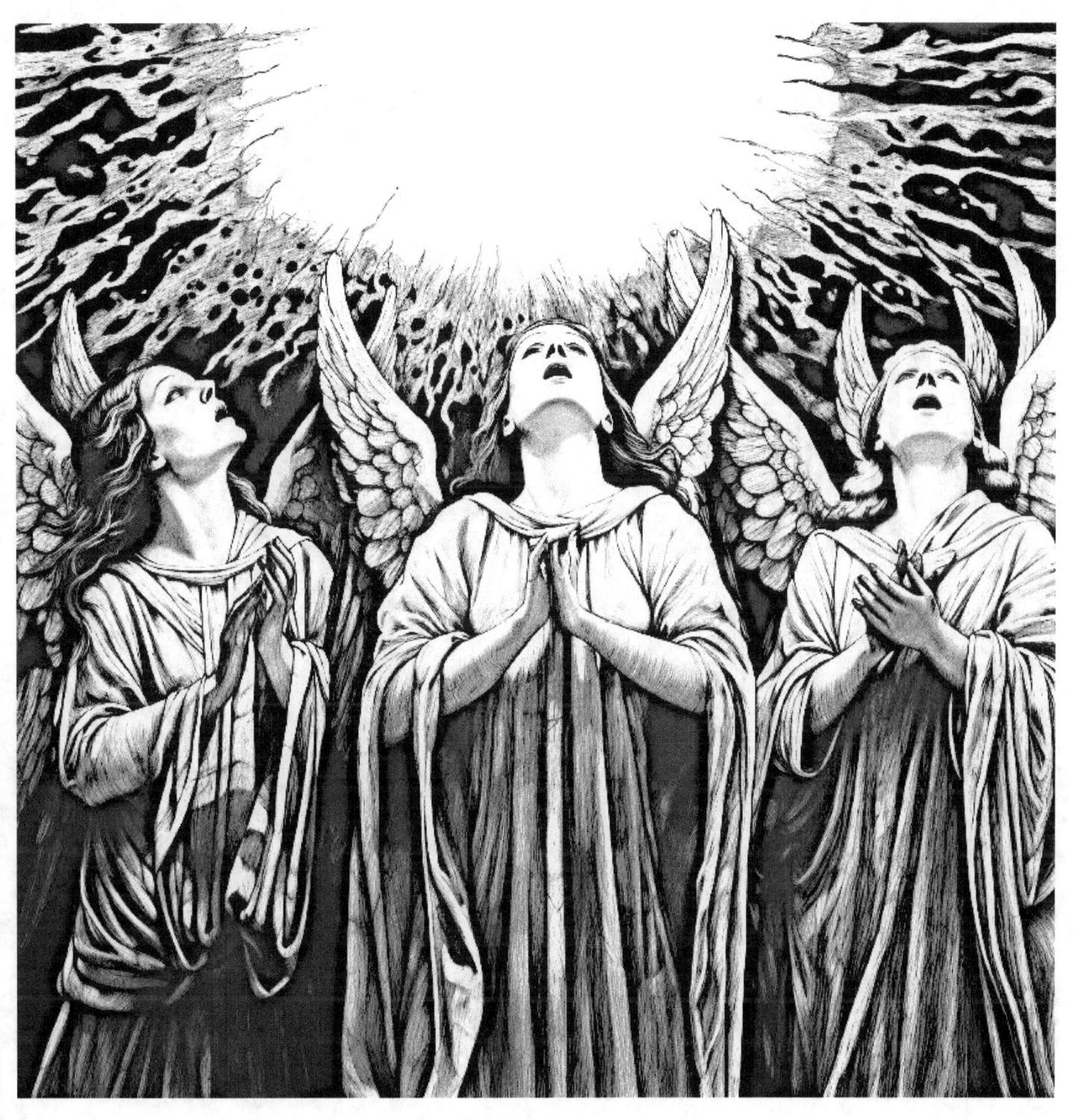

Psalm 91:11 KJV

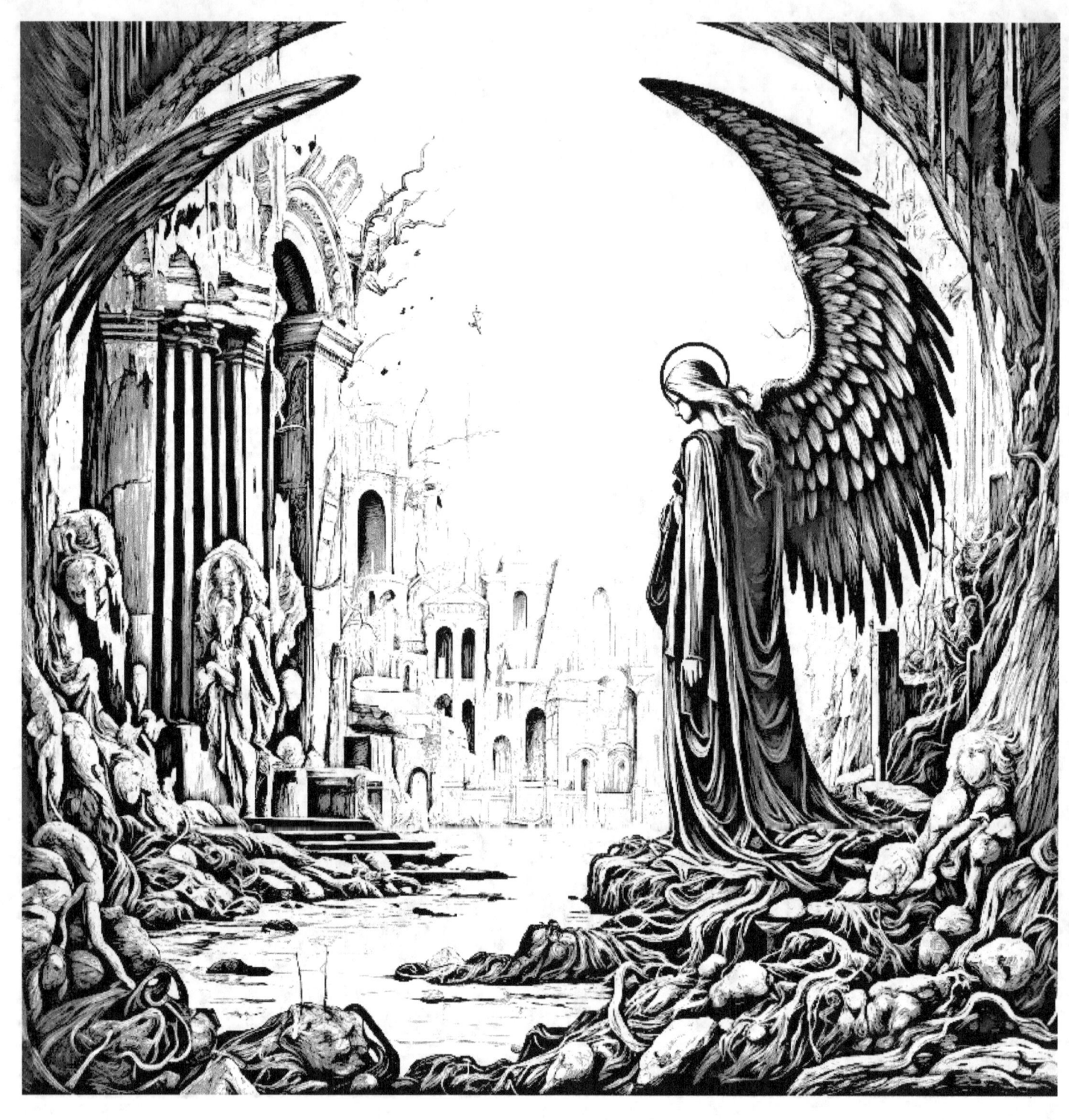

Psalm 91:11-12

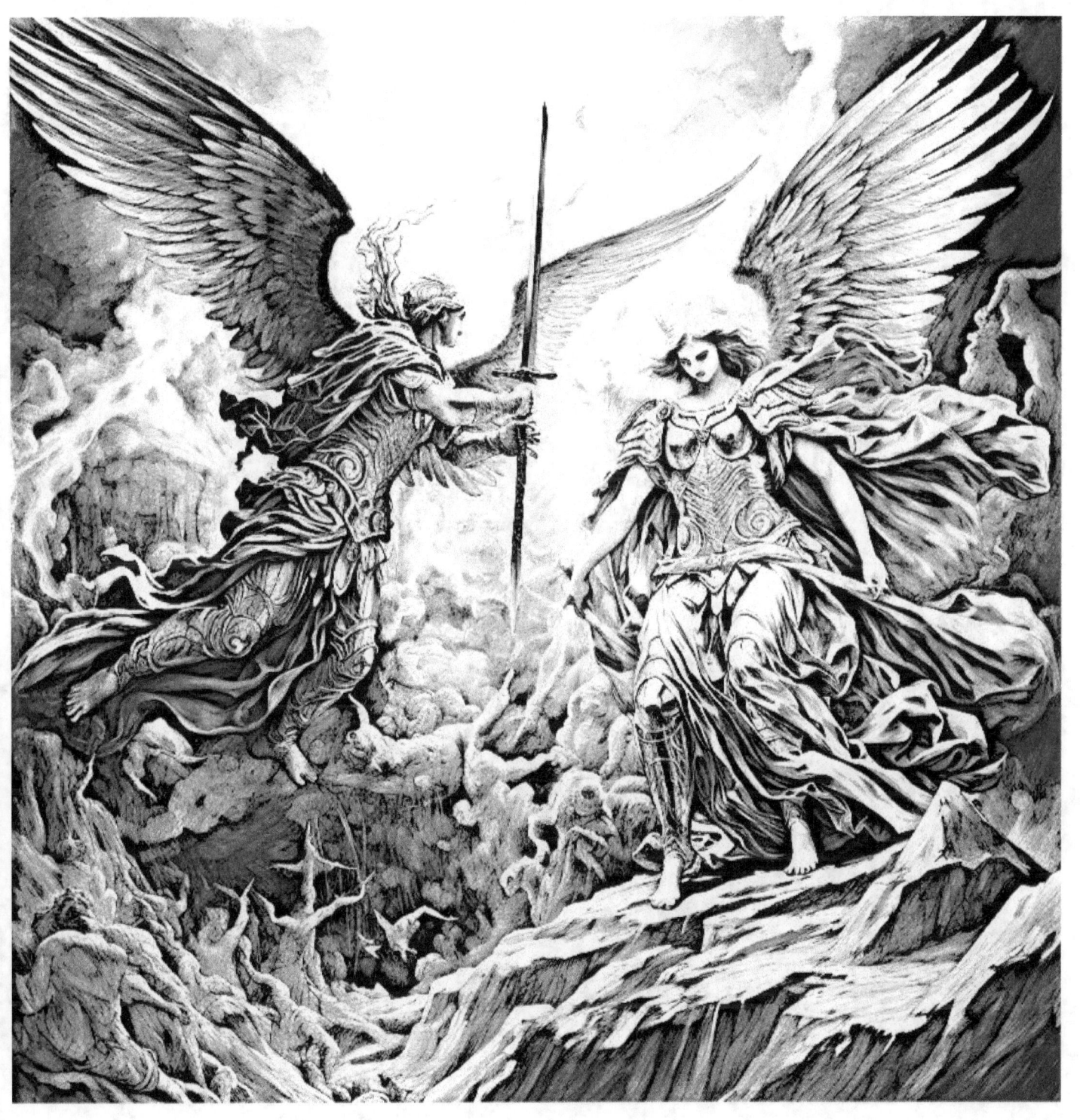

Matthew 4:11

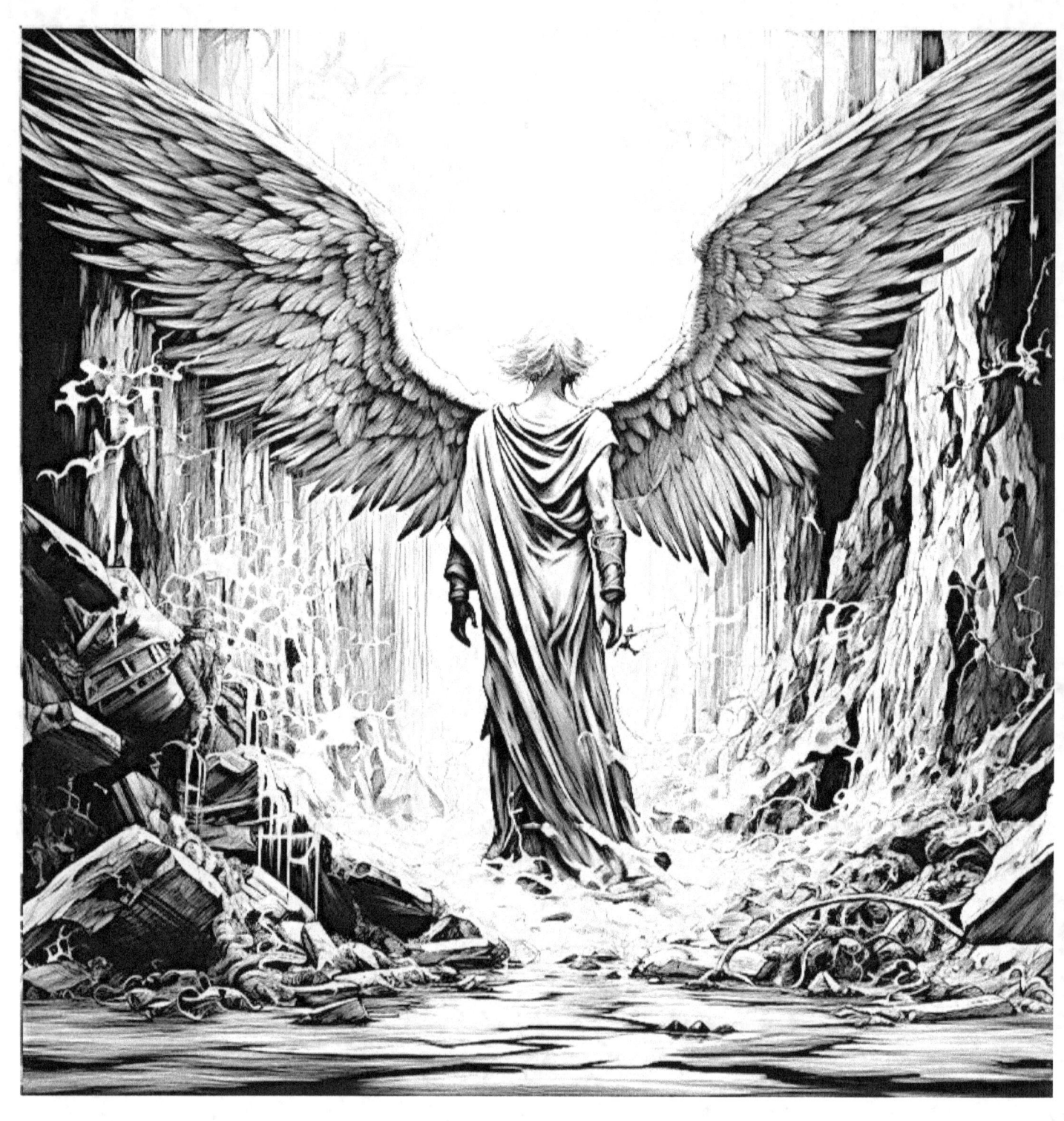

Daniel 6:22

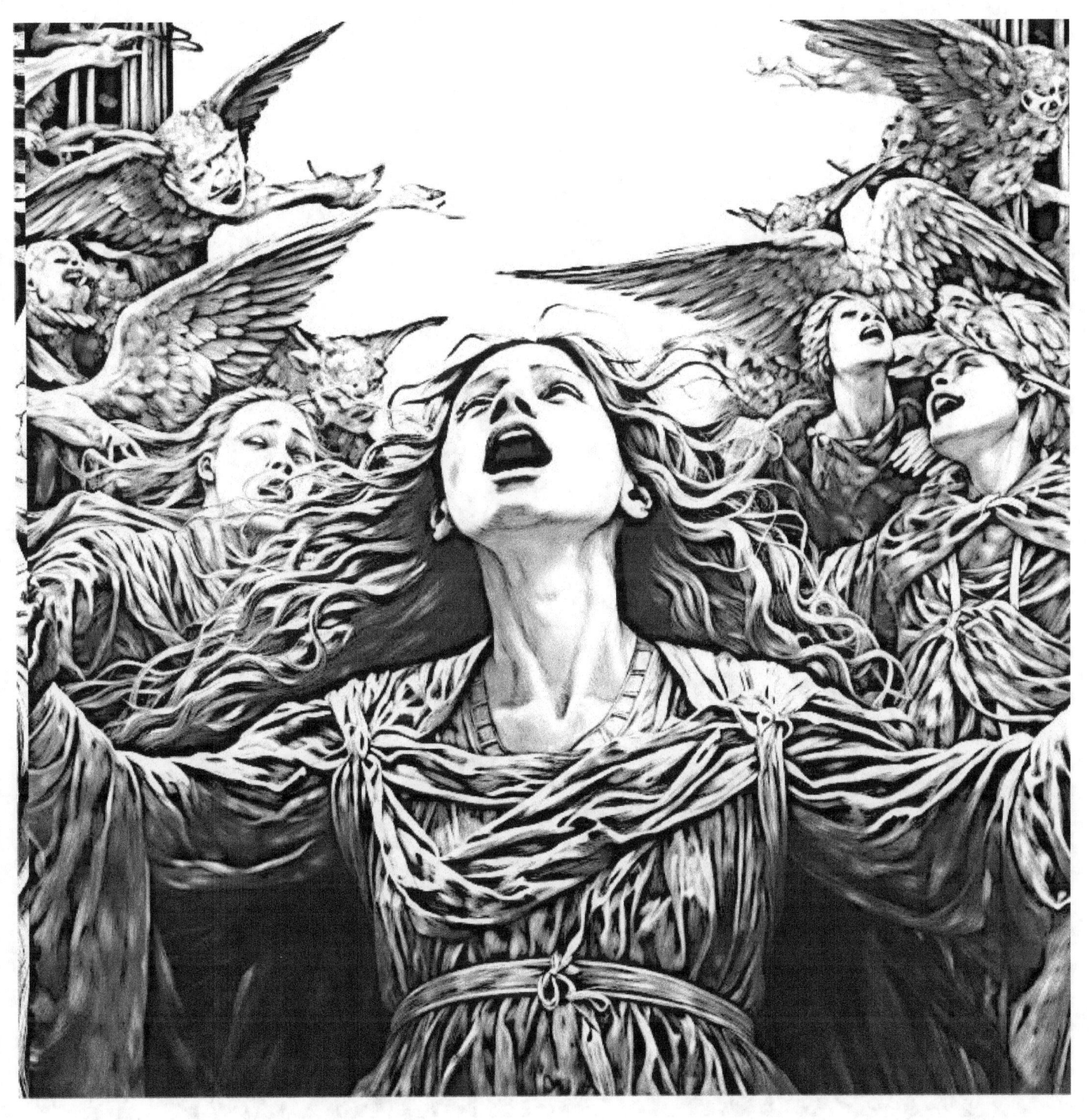

Ezekiel 10:4-5

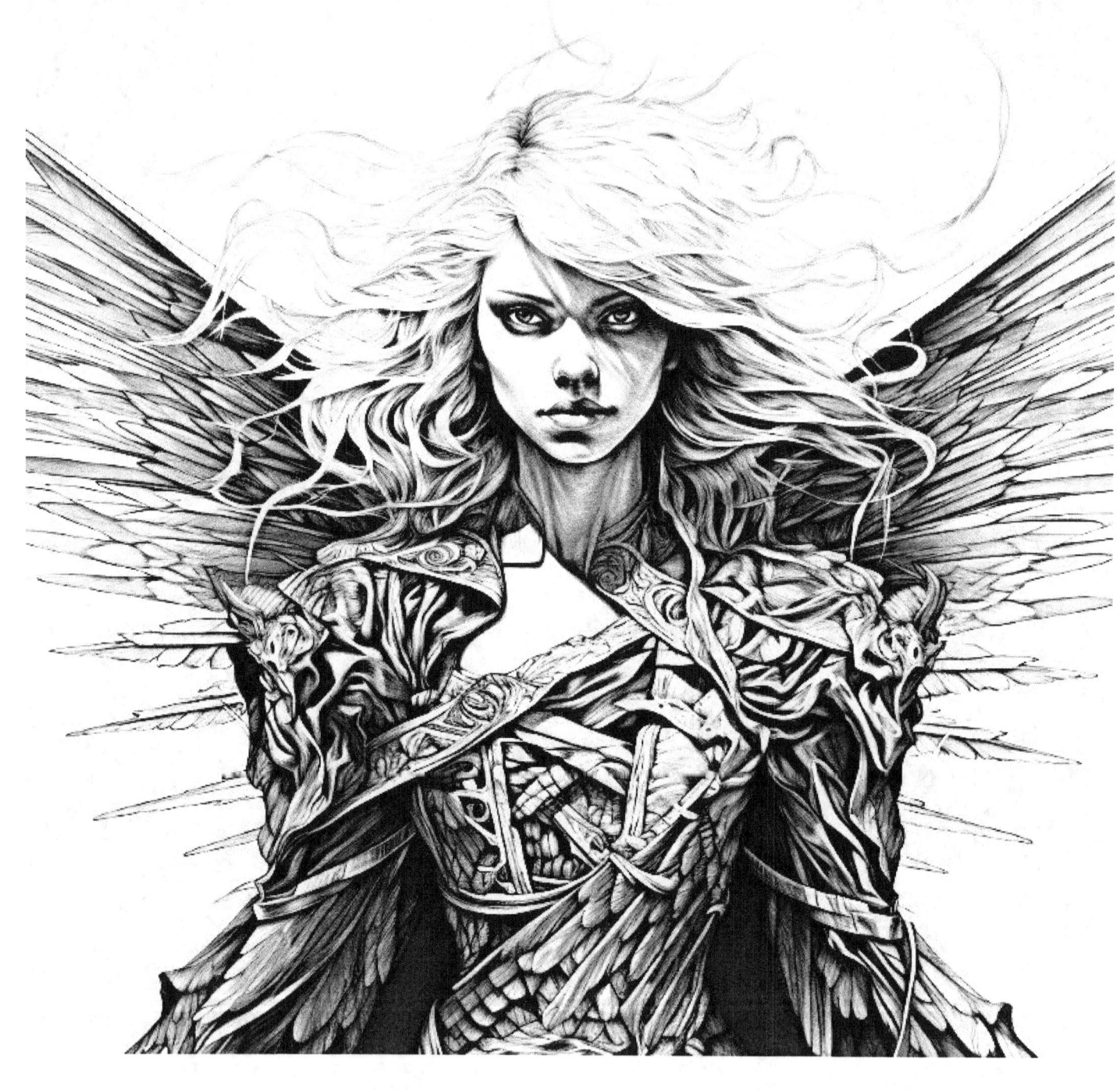

Matthew 28:2-7

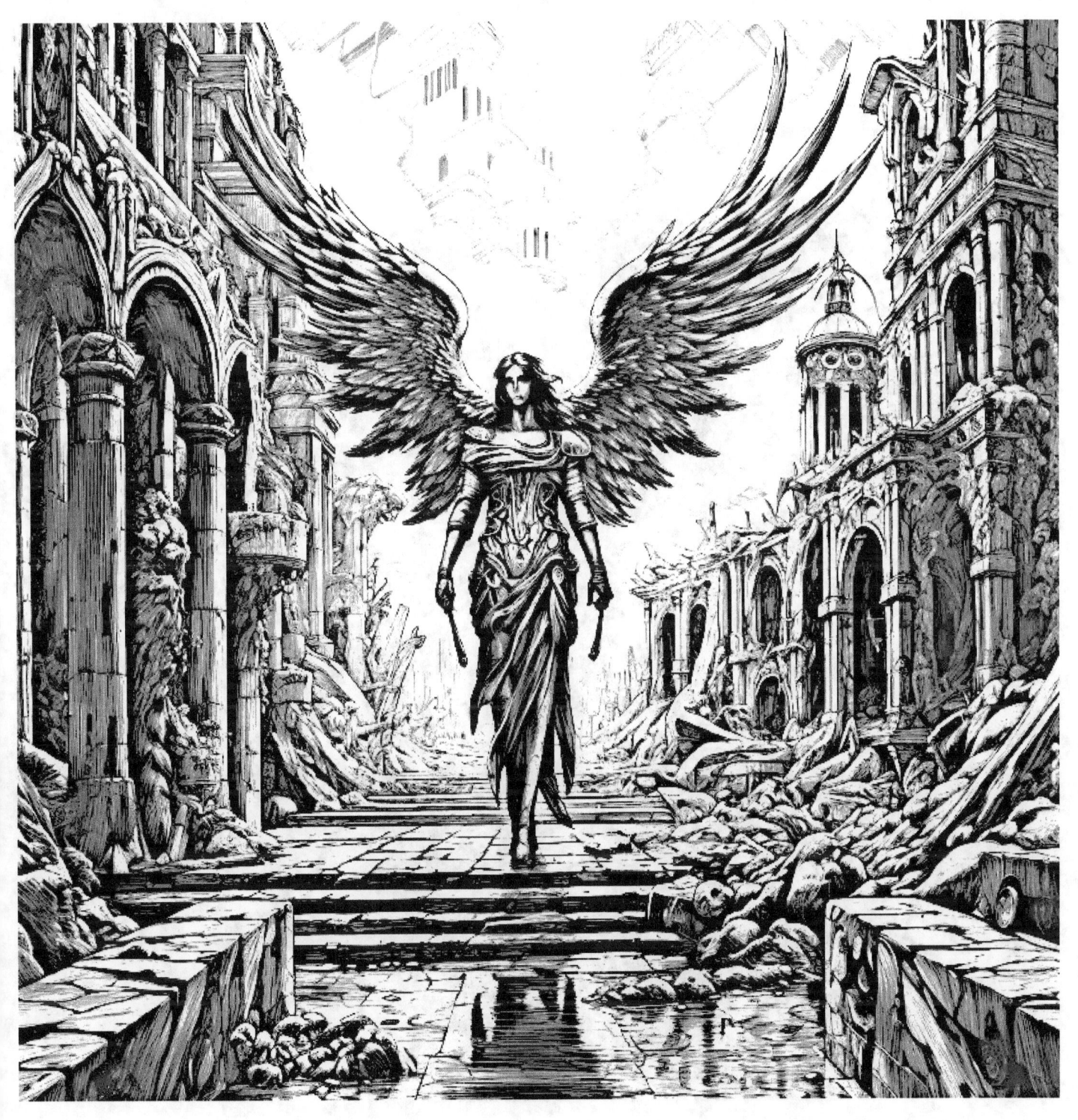

Psalm 35:5

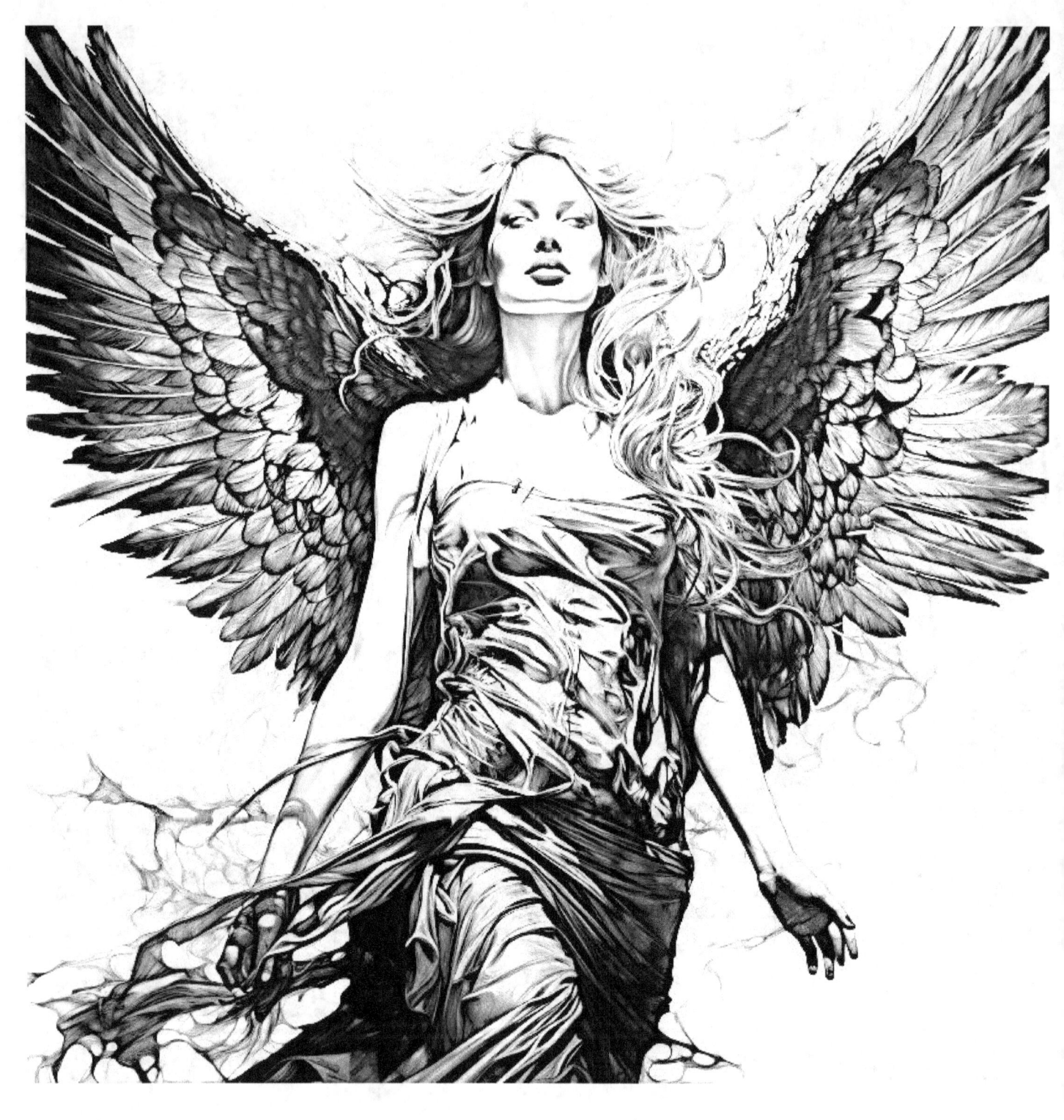

Revelation 22:8

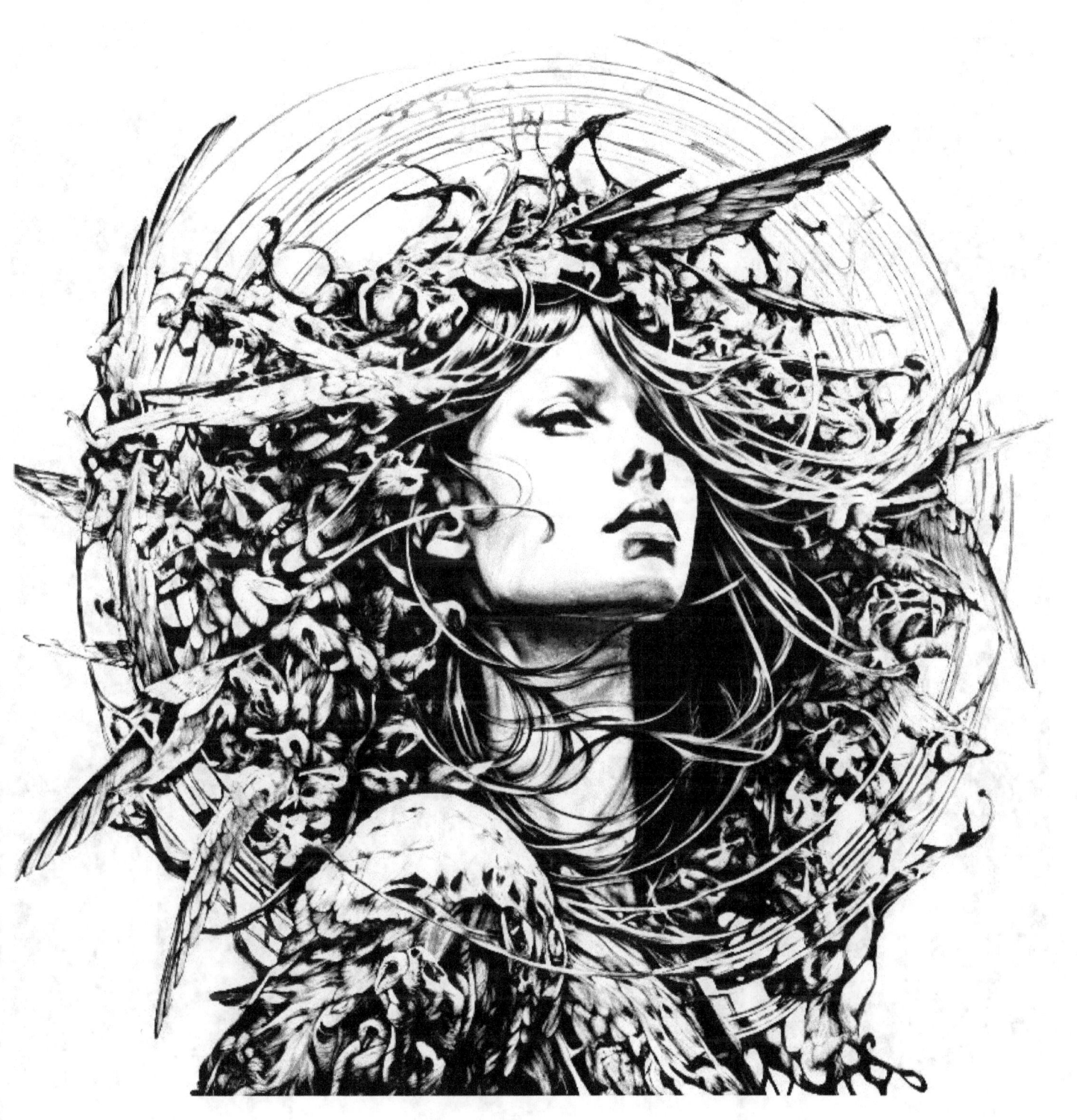

Isaiah 63:9

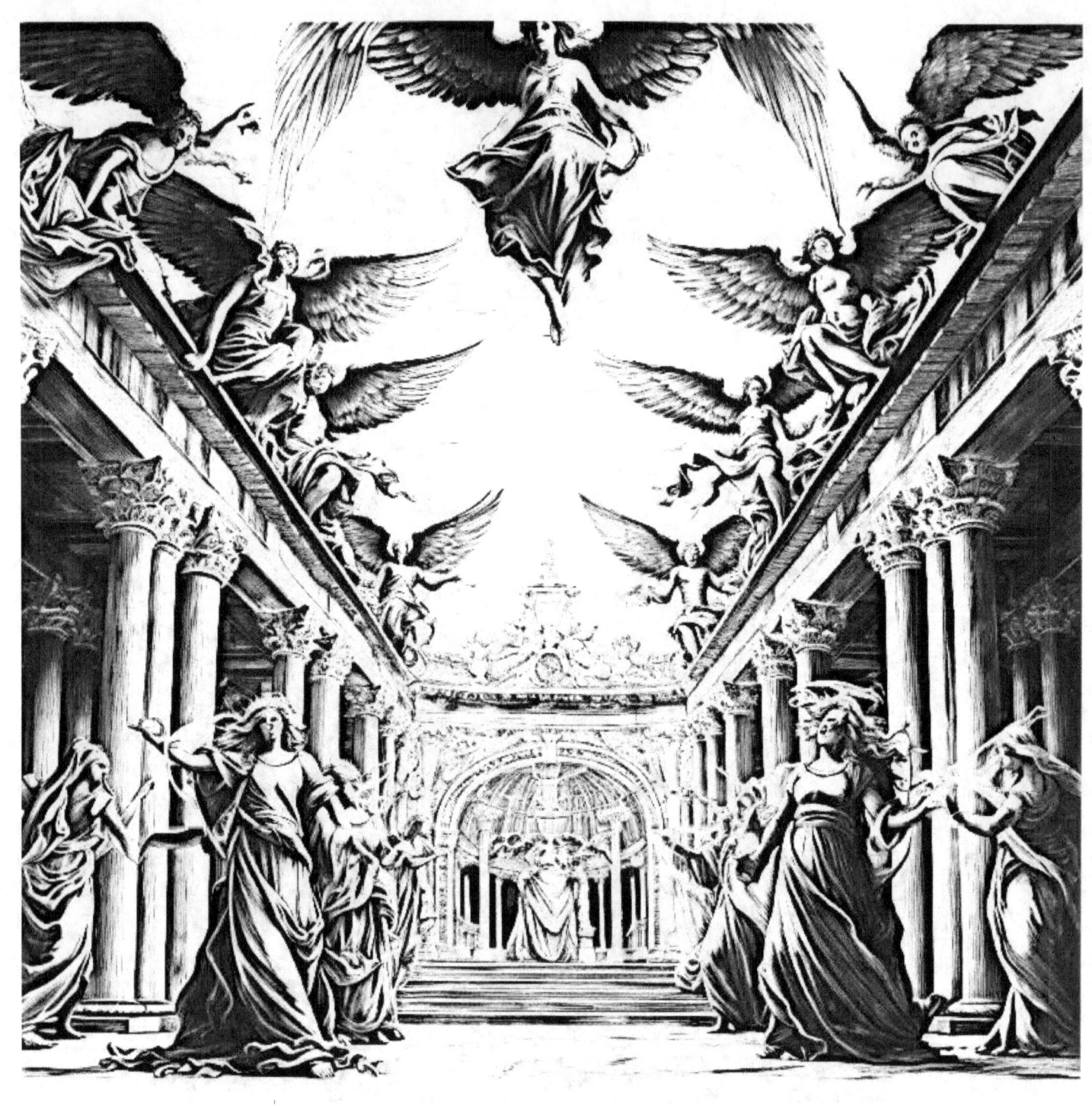

Isaiah 37:16

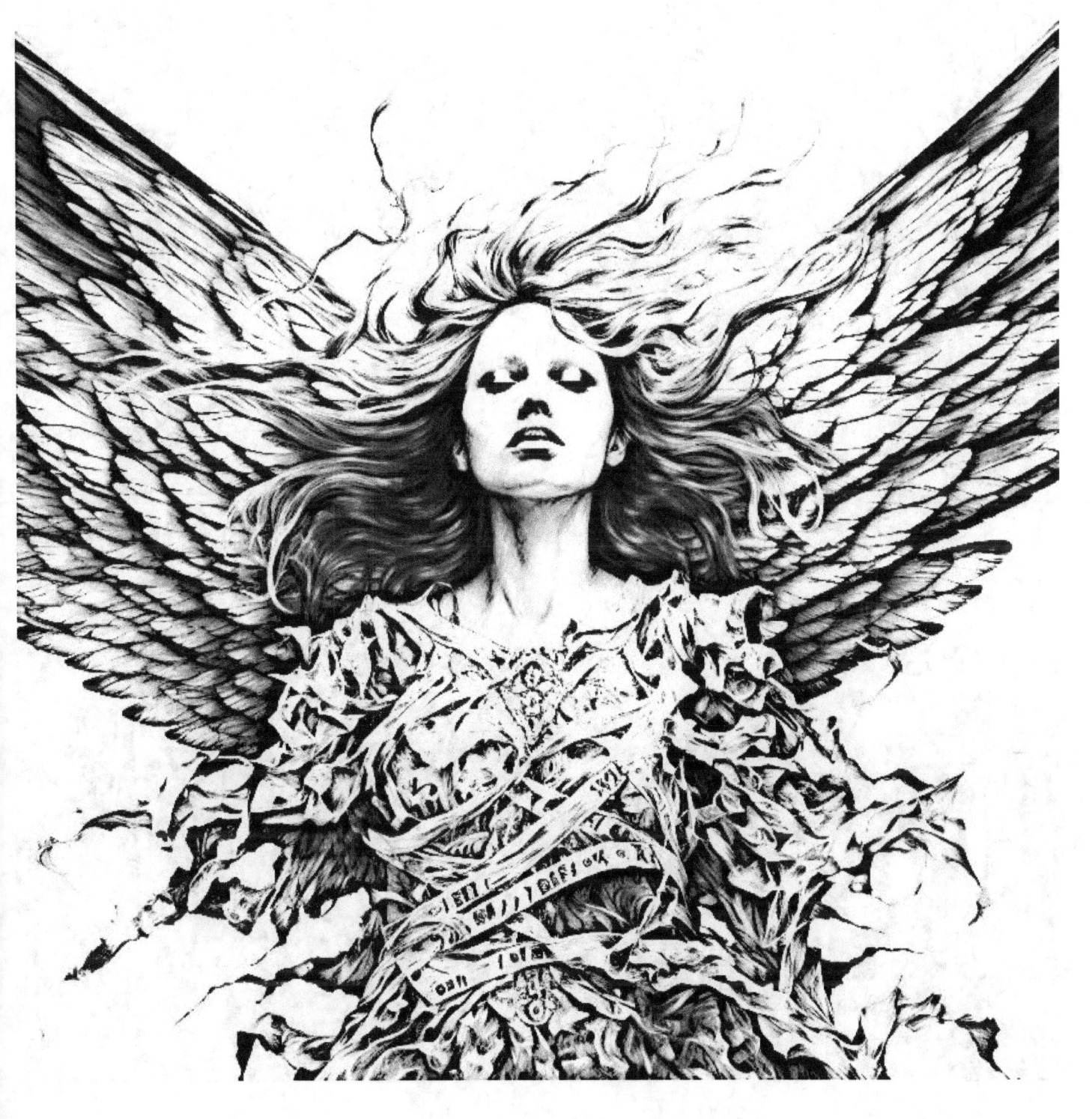

Luke 4:10

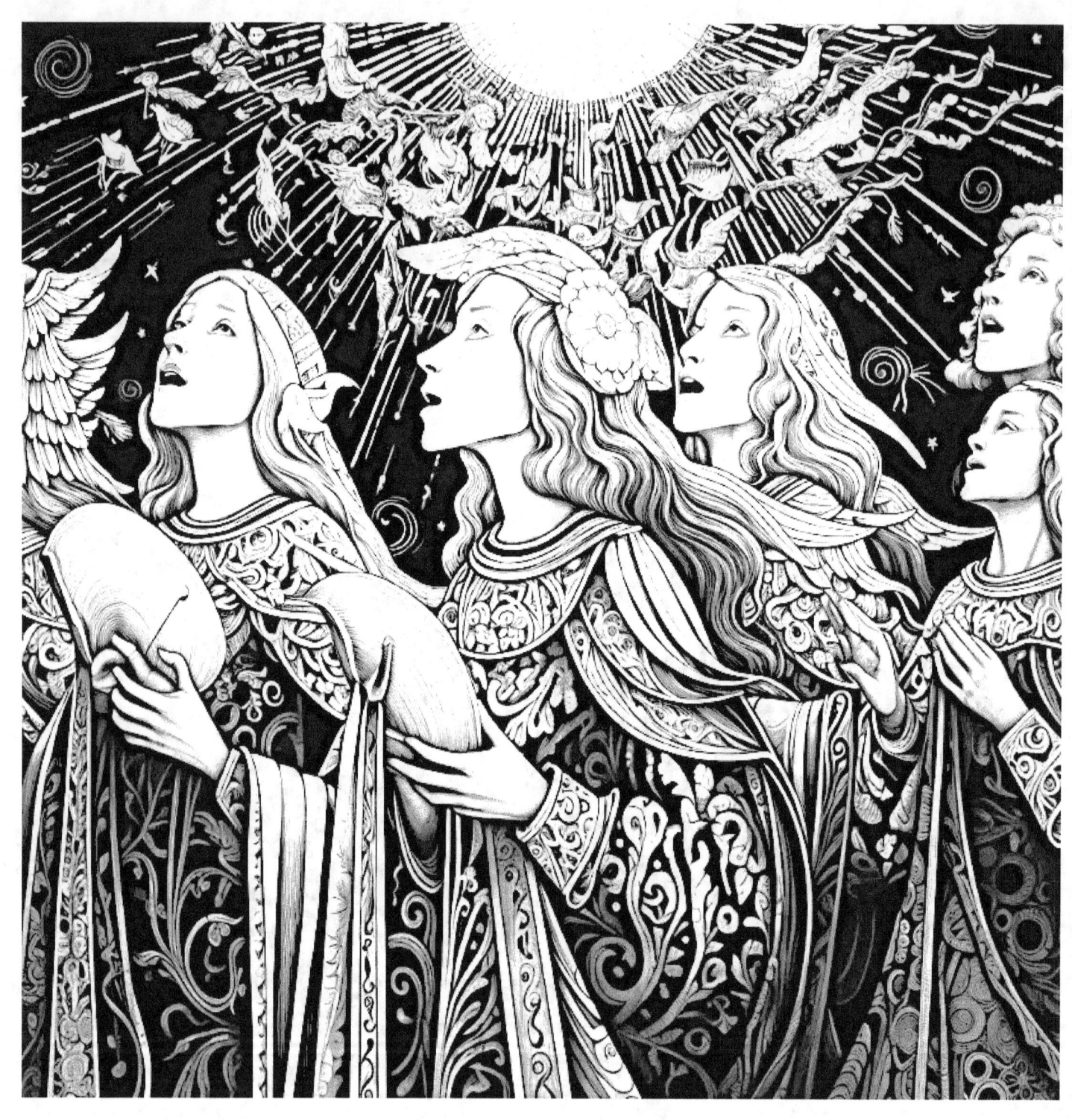

Psalm 80:1

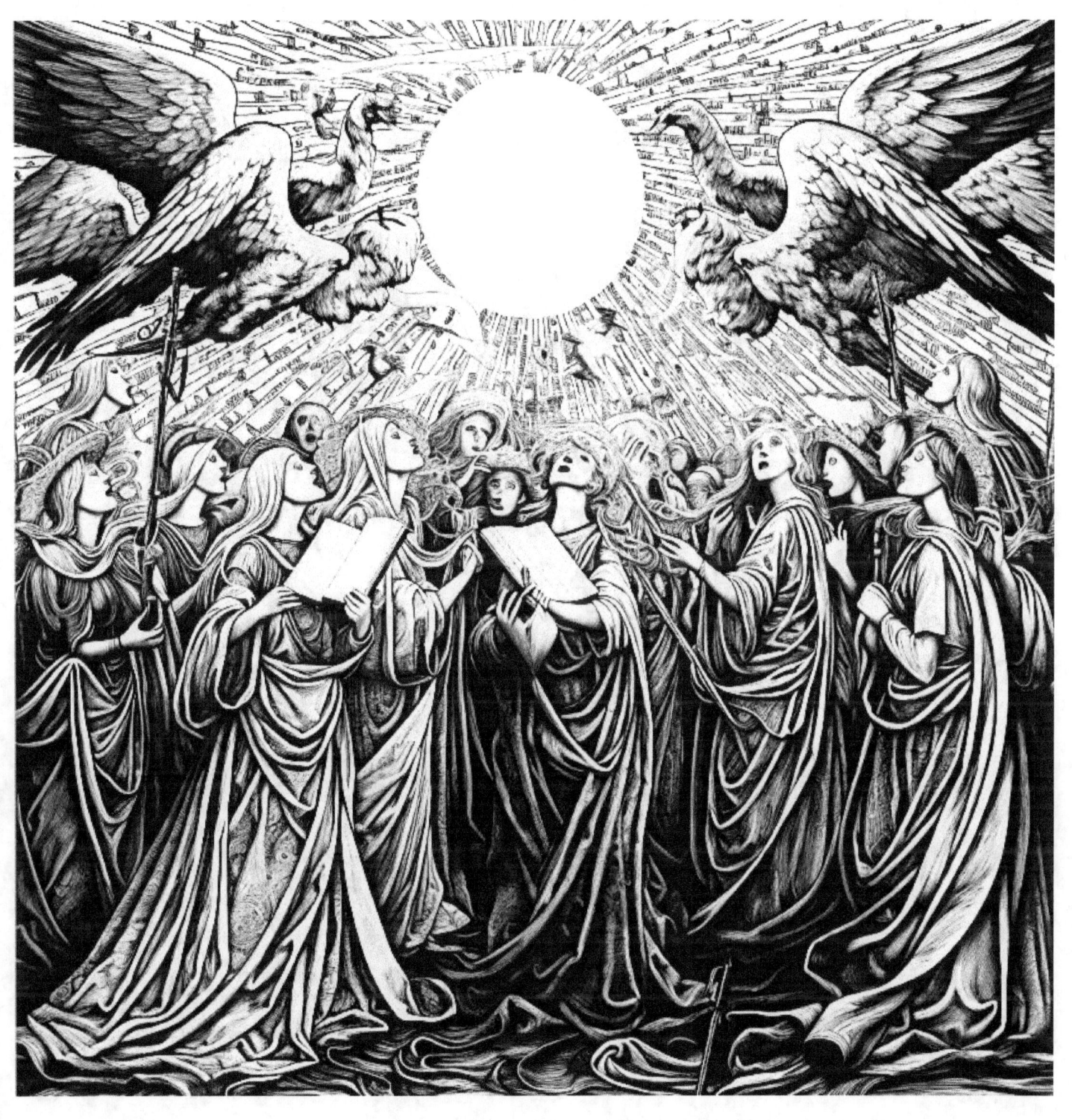

Matthew 24:31-35

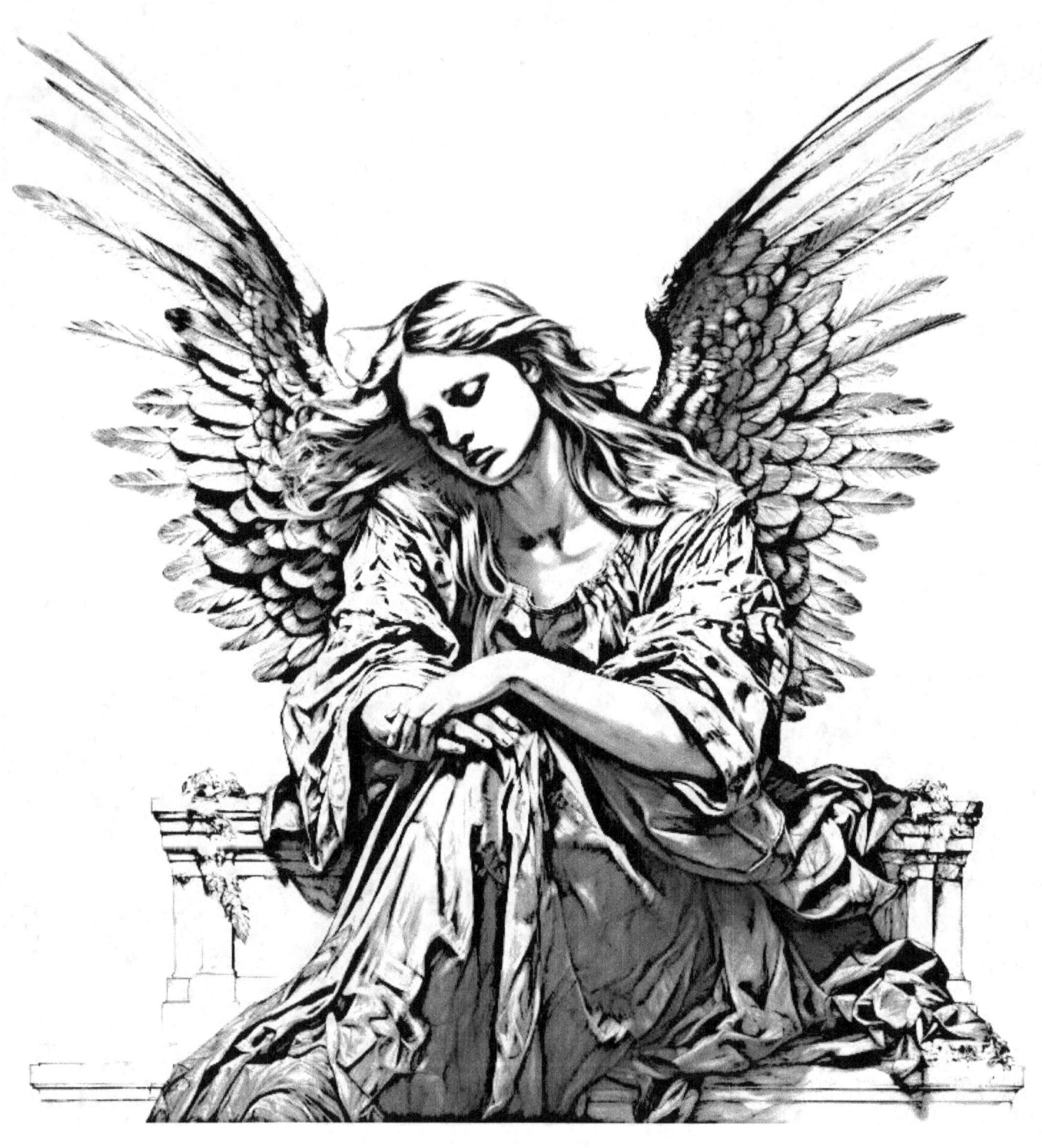

2 peter 2:4

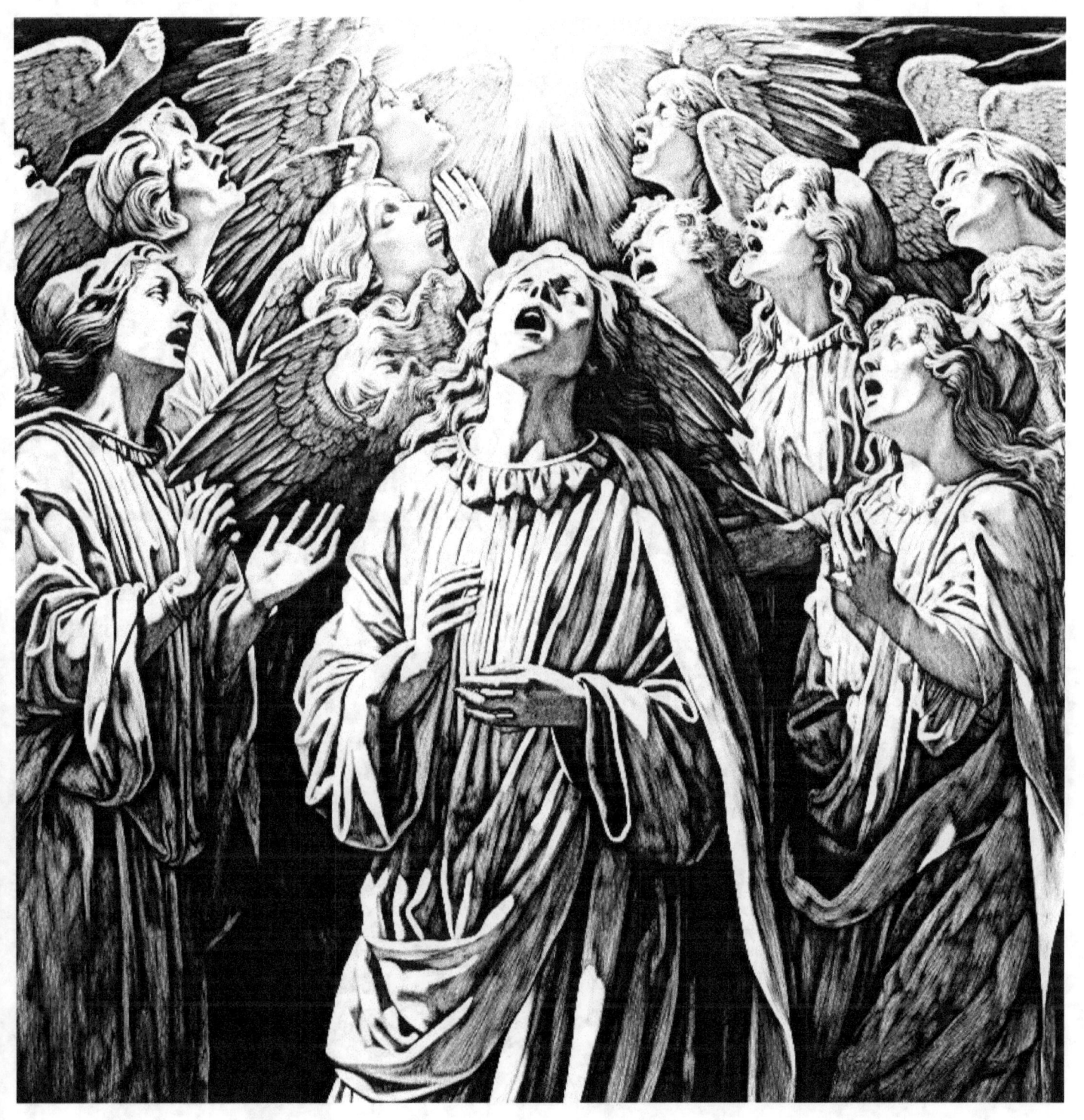

Matthew 25:31

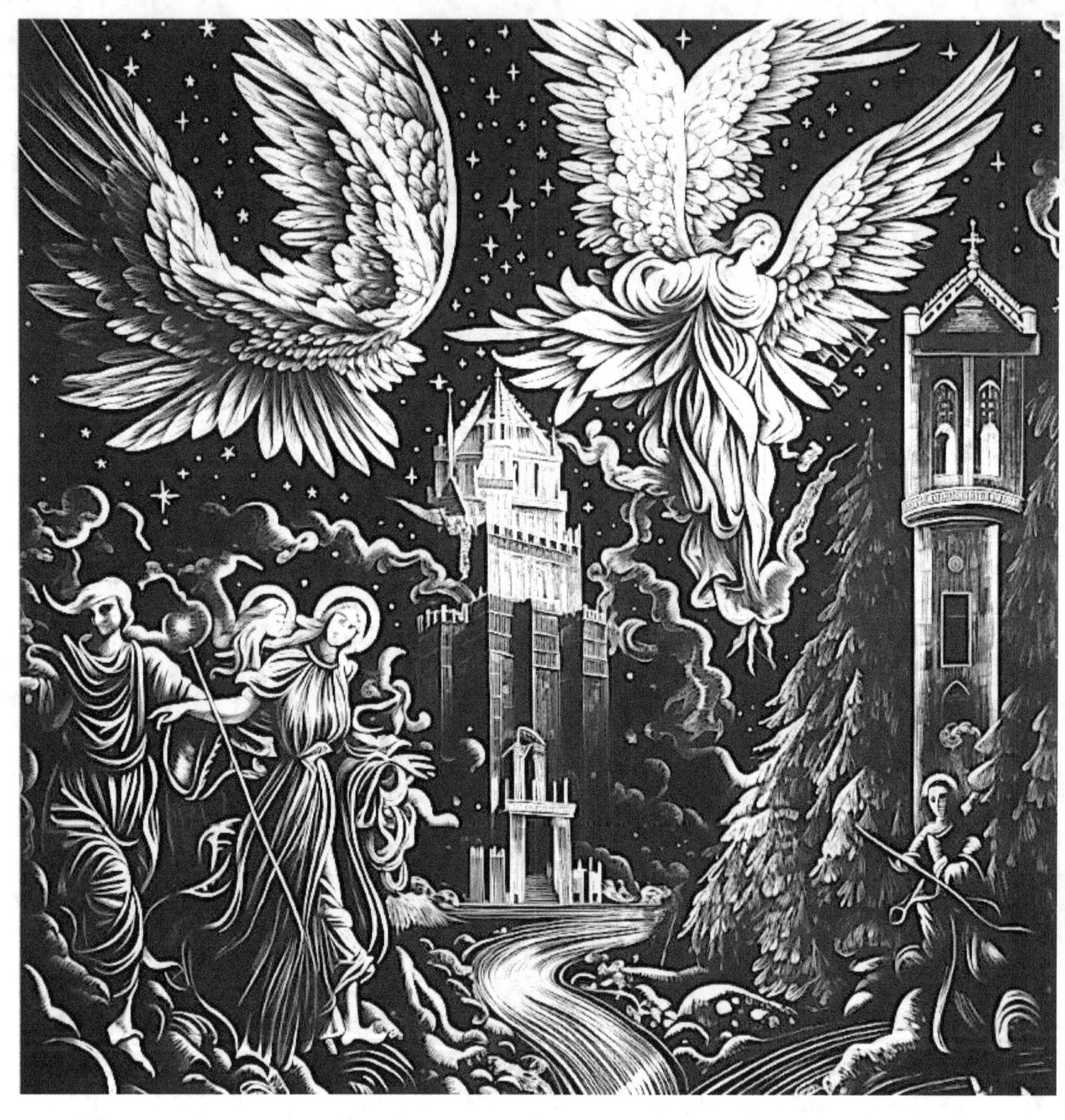

Matthew 4:6-11

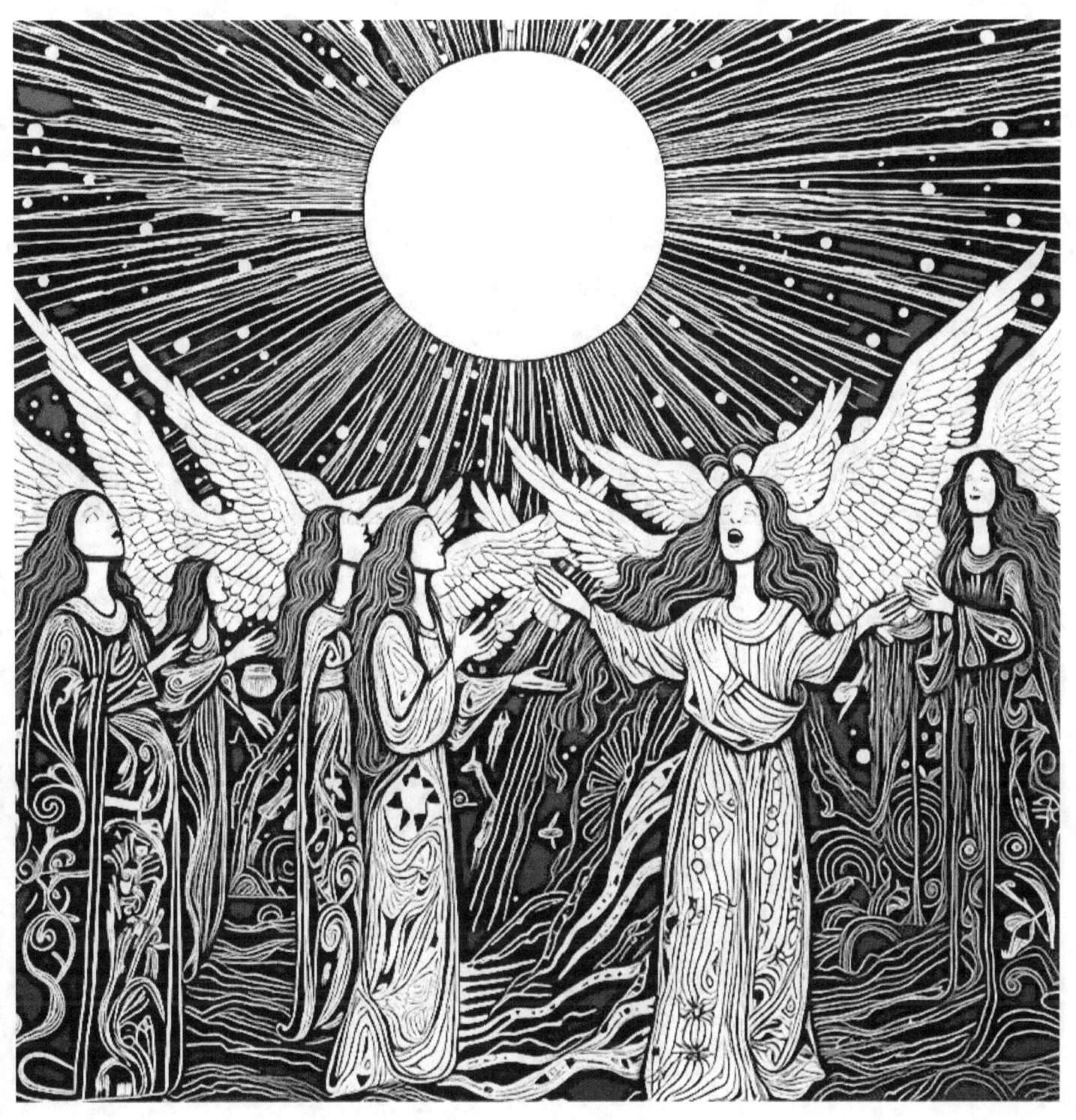

Psalm 68:17

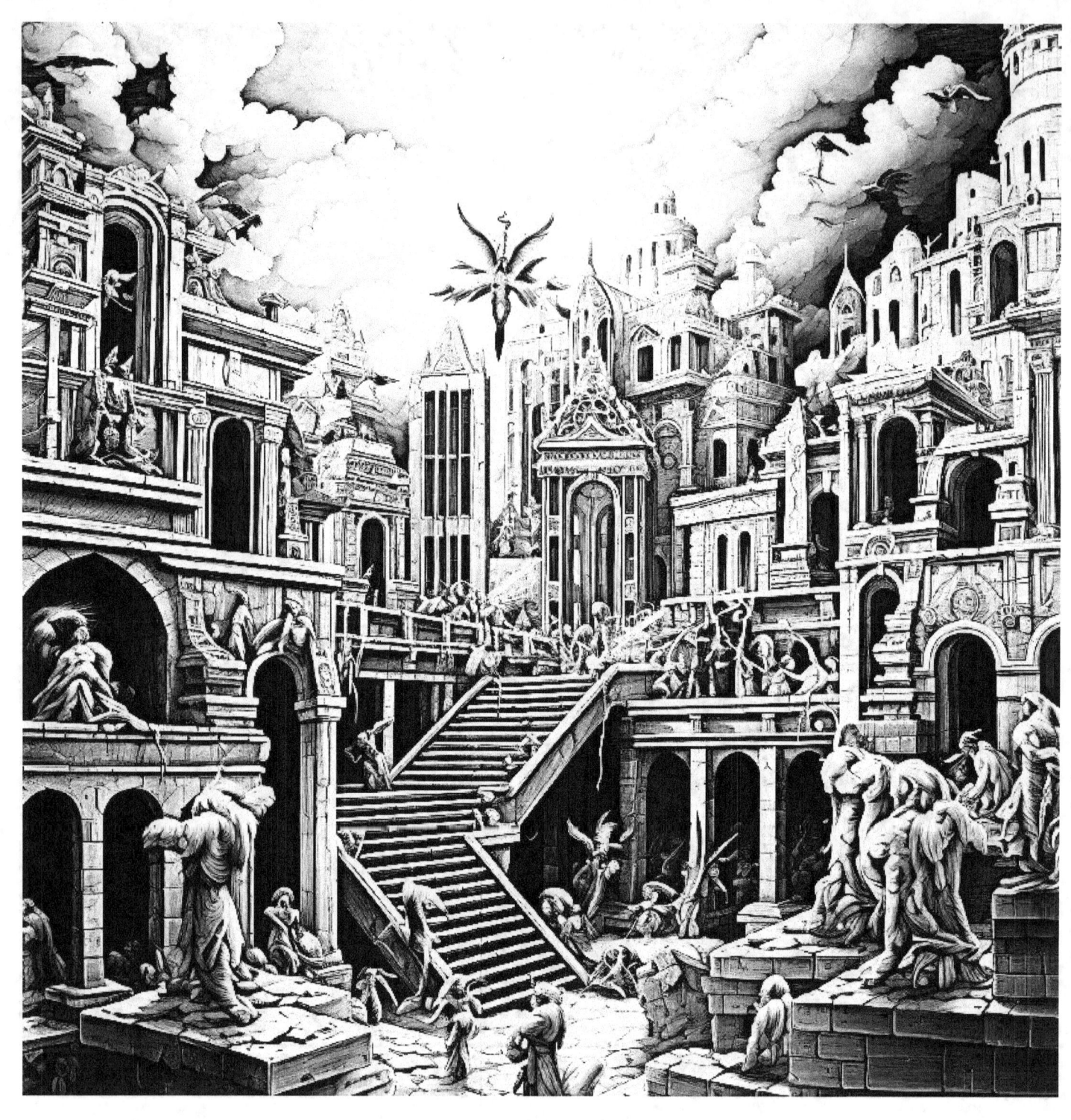

Psalm 103:19-22

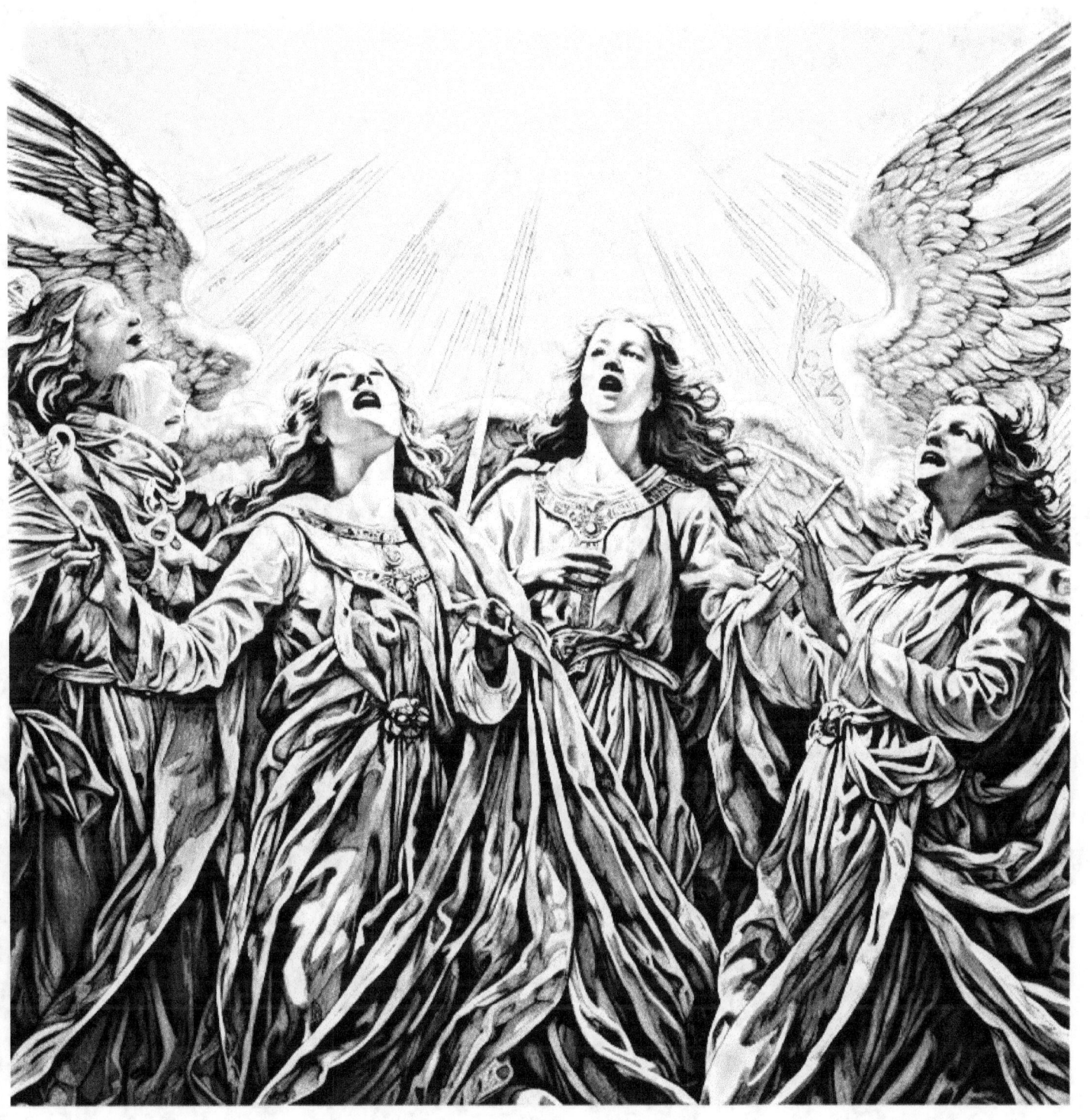

Matthew 22:30

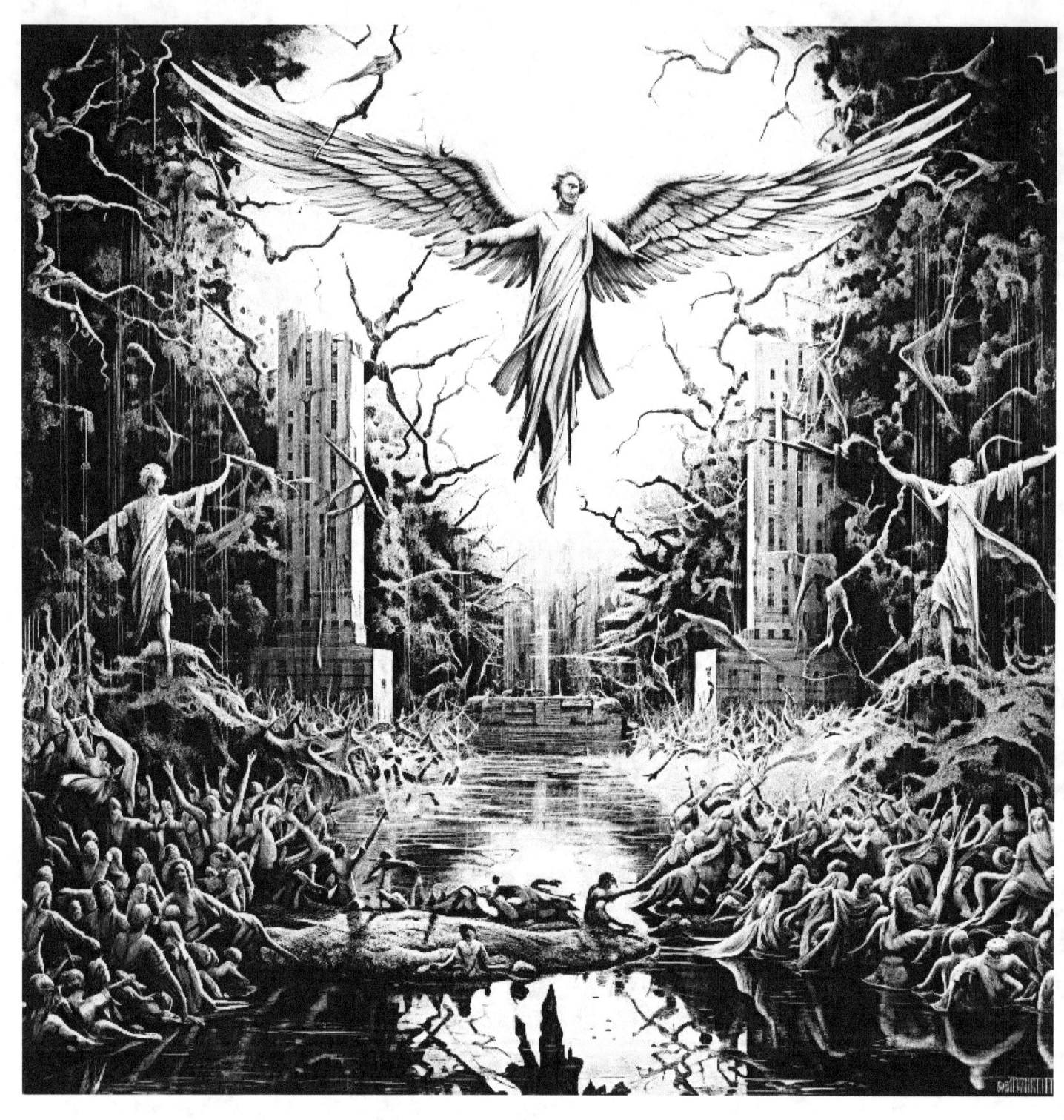

Matthew 28:5-6

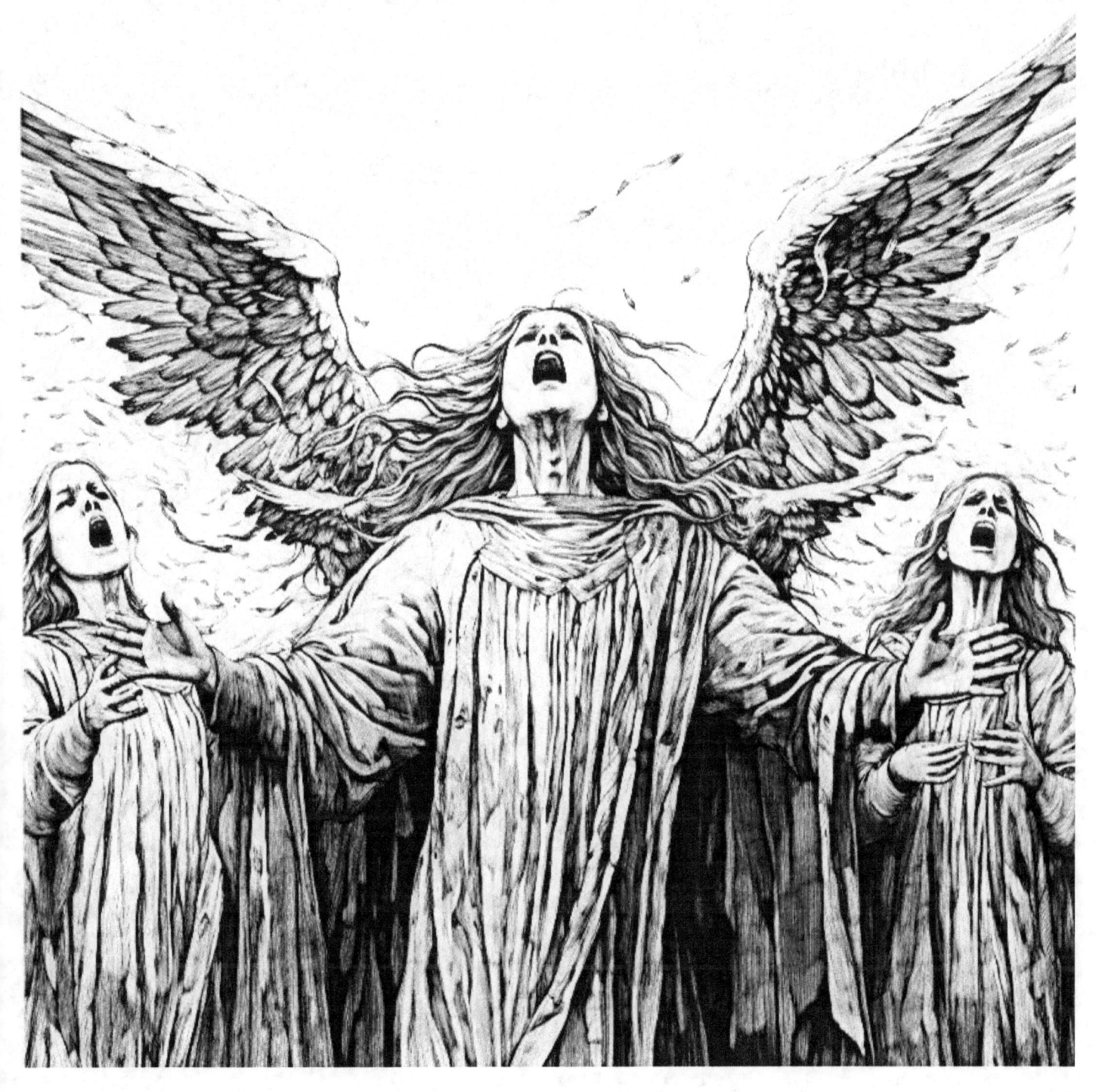

Hebrews 13:1-2

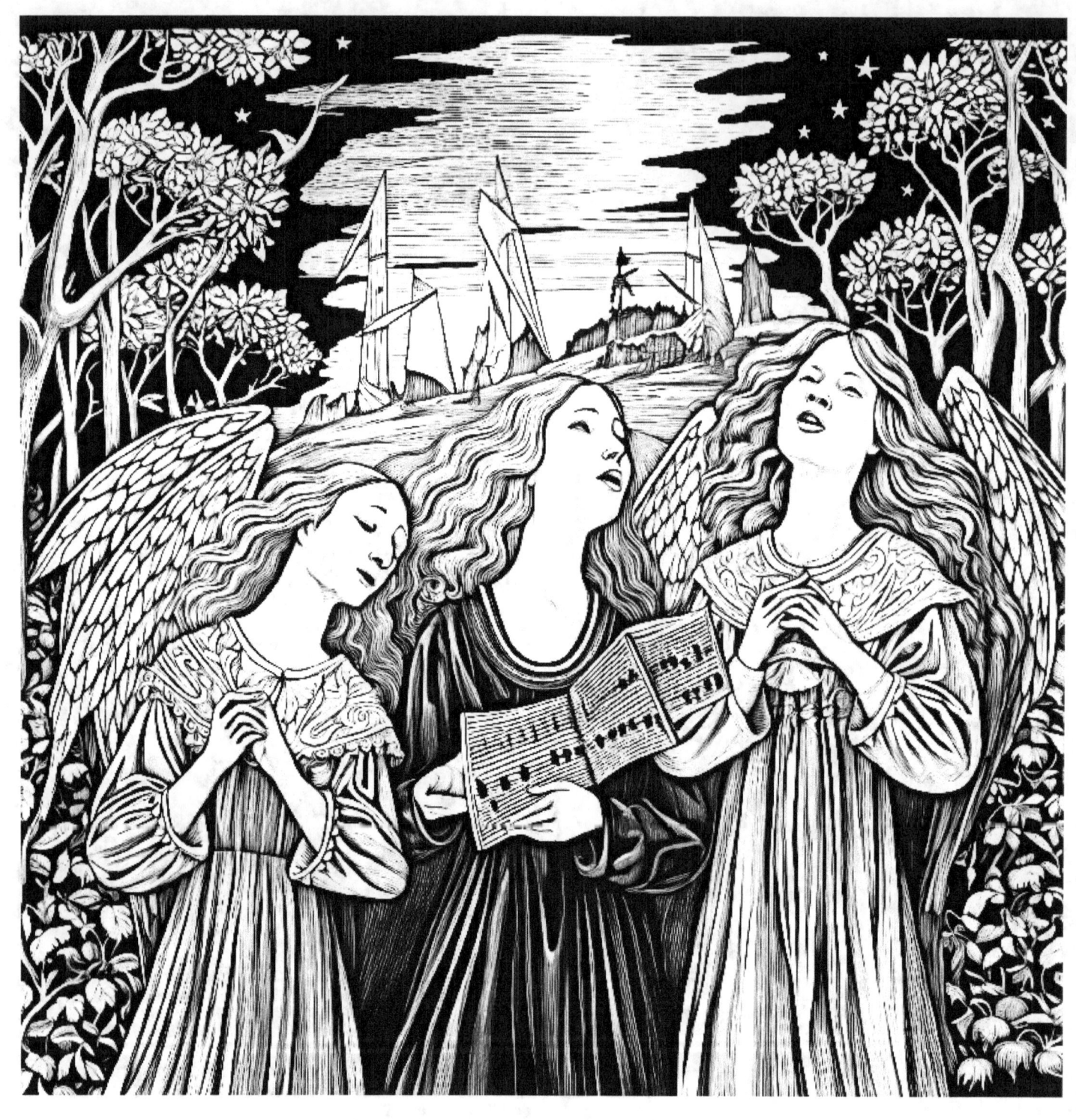

Revelation 5:11

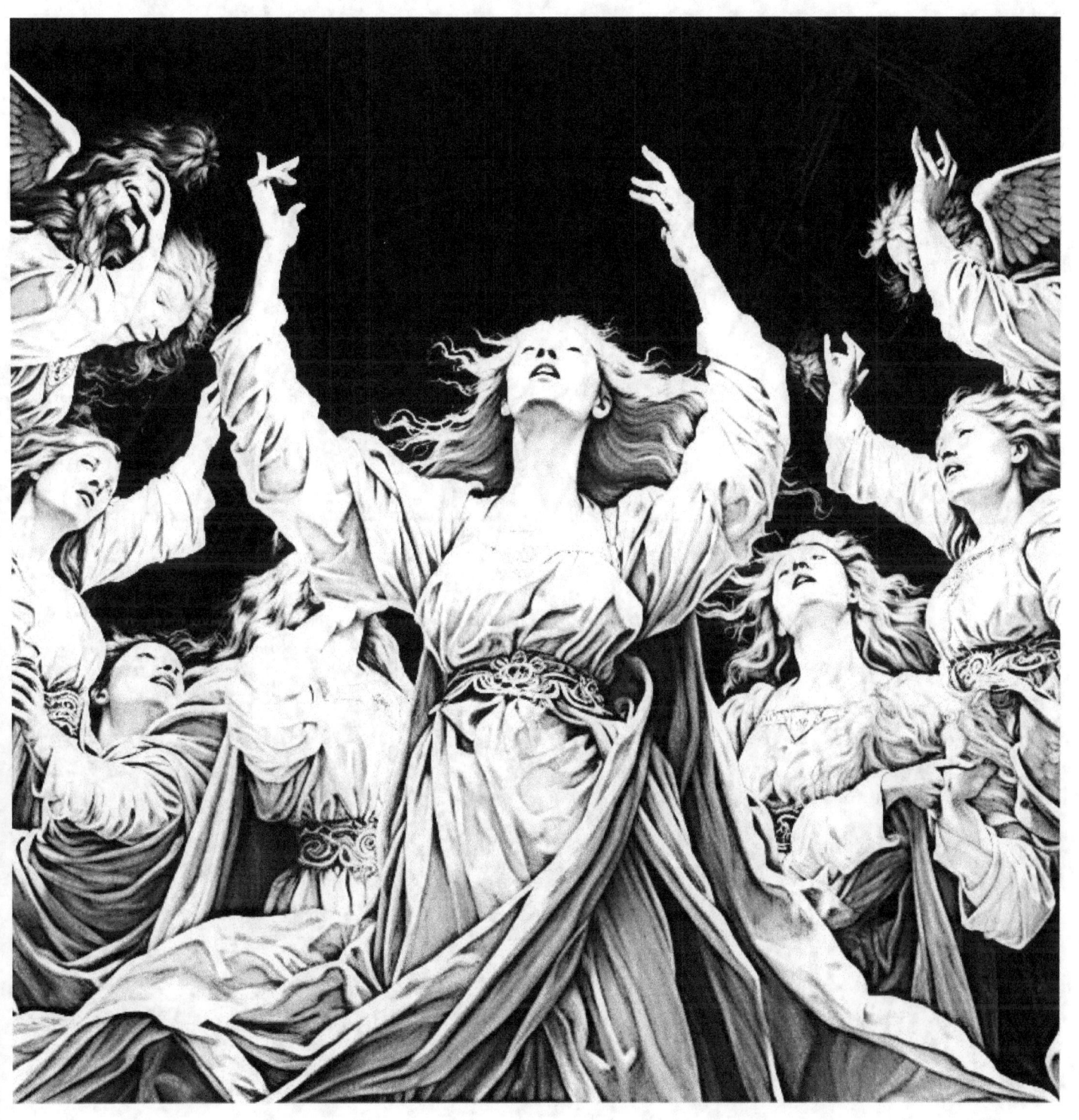

1 John 4:1

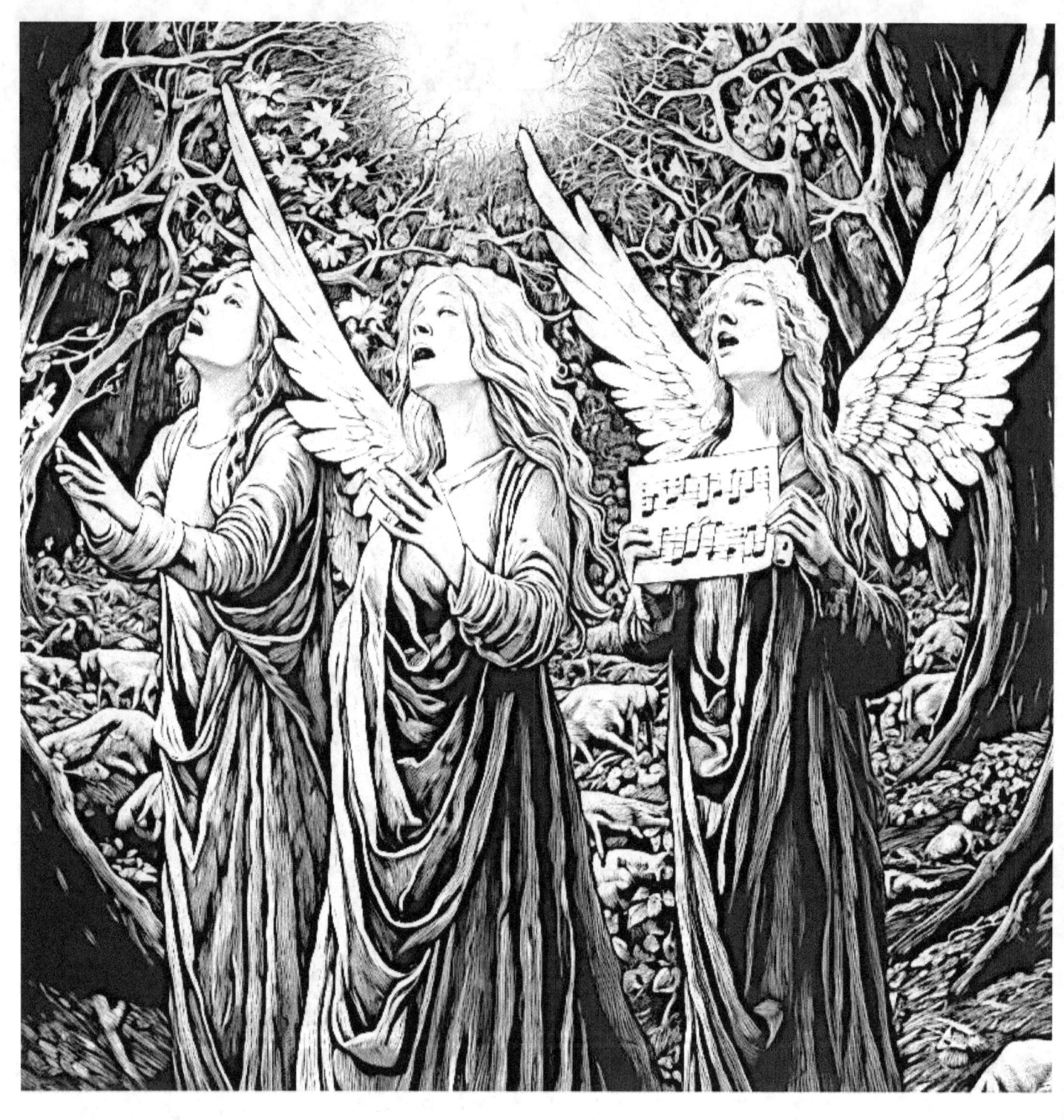

Hebrews 1:7

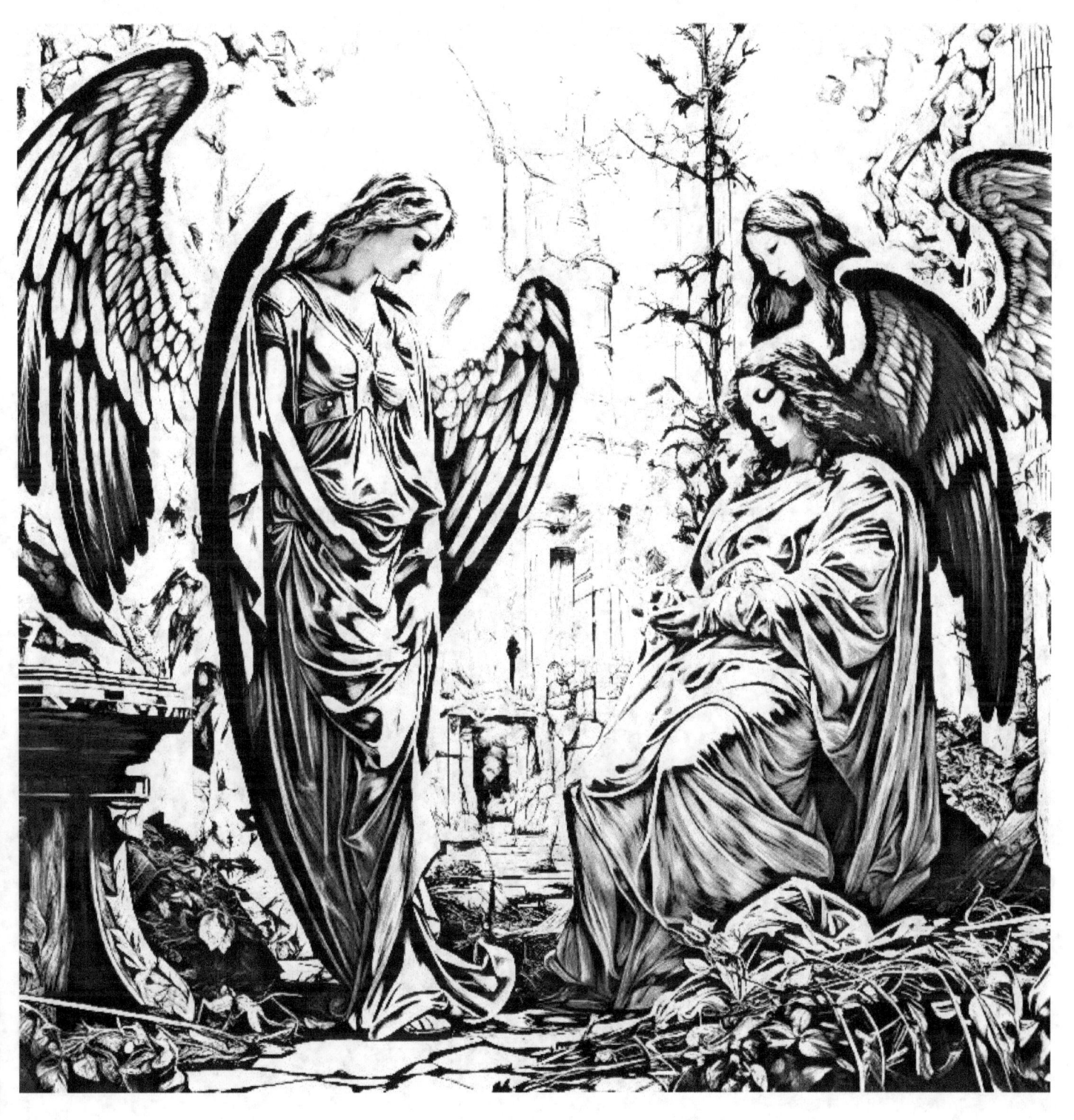

1 Timothy 5:21

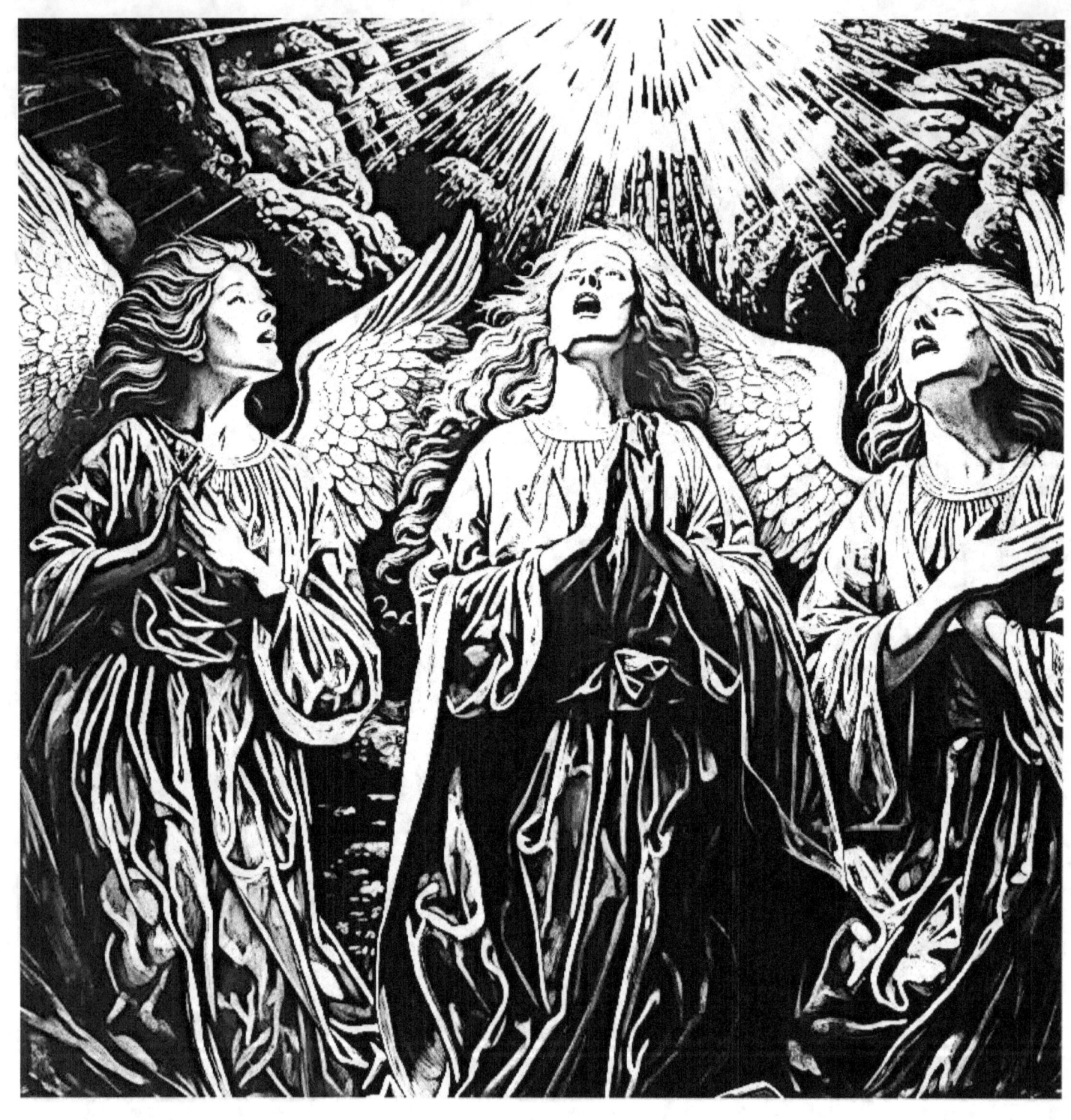

Matthew 24:36

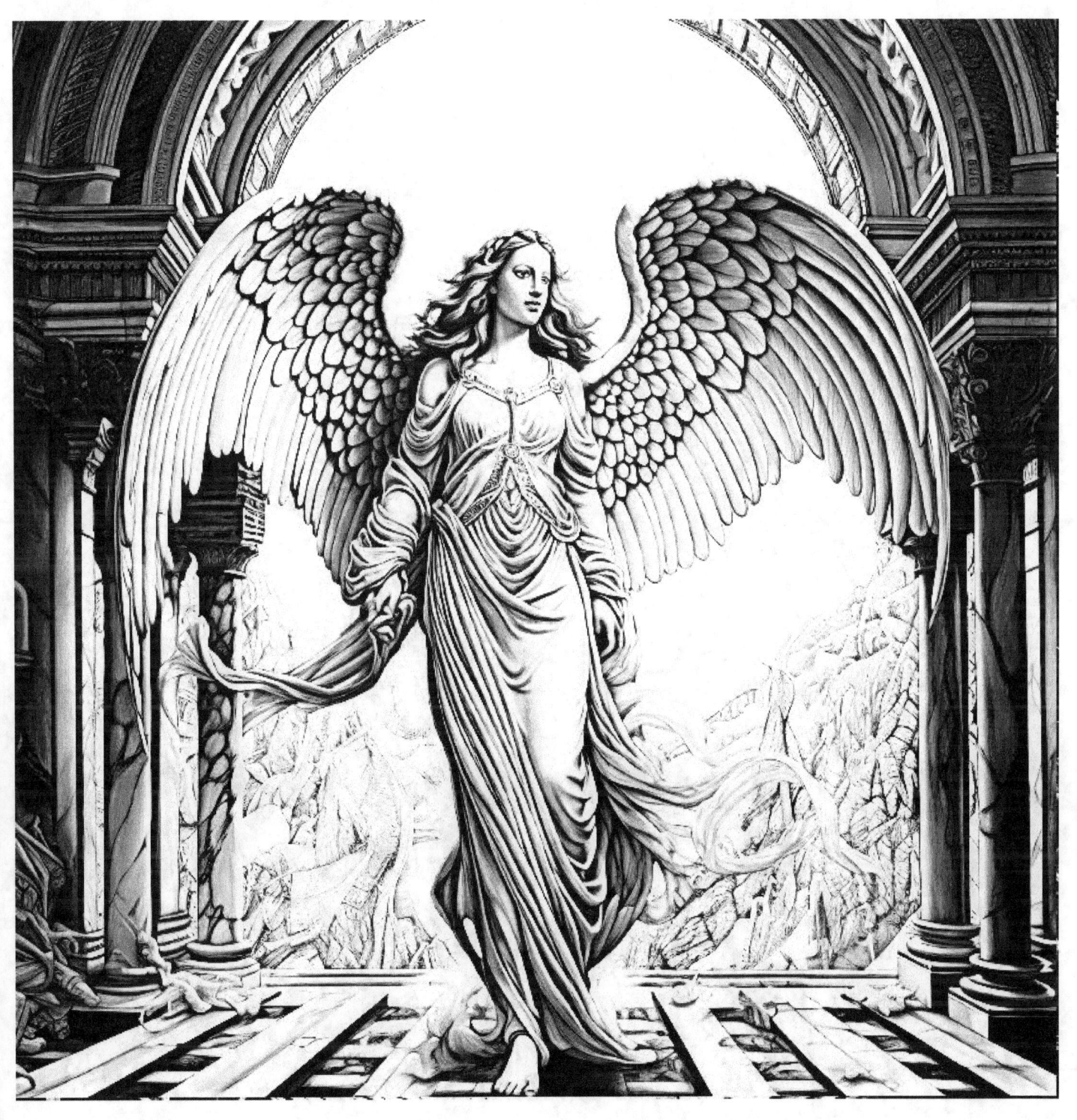

Genesis 28:12

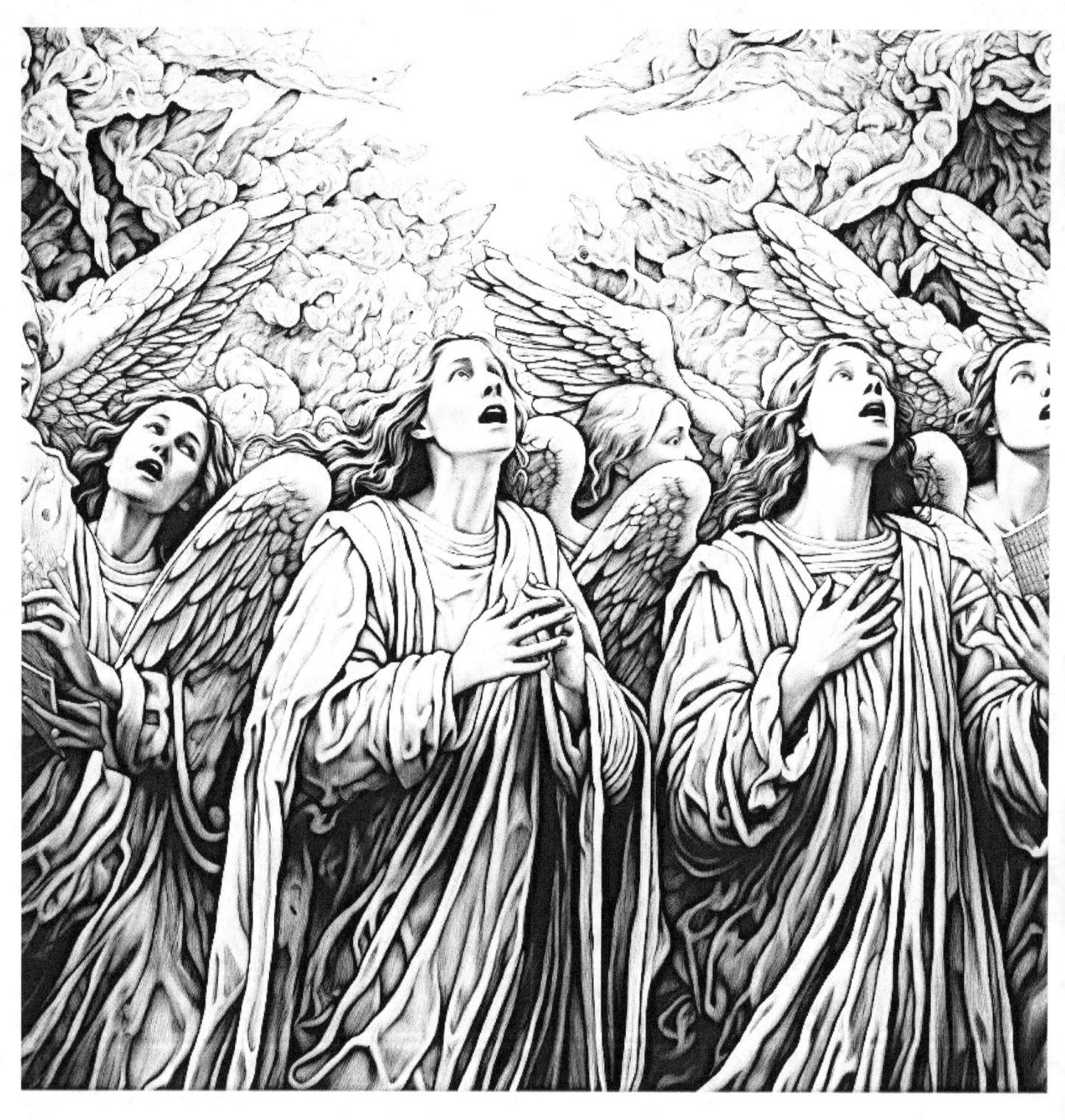

1 Peter 1:12

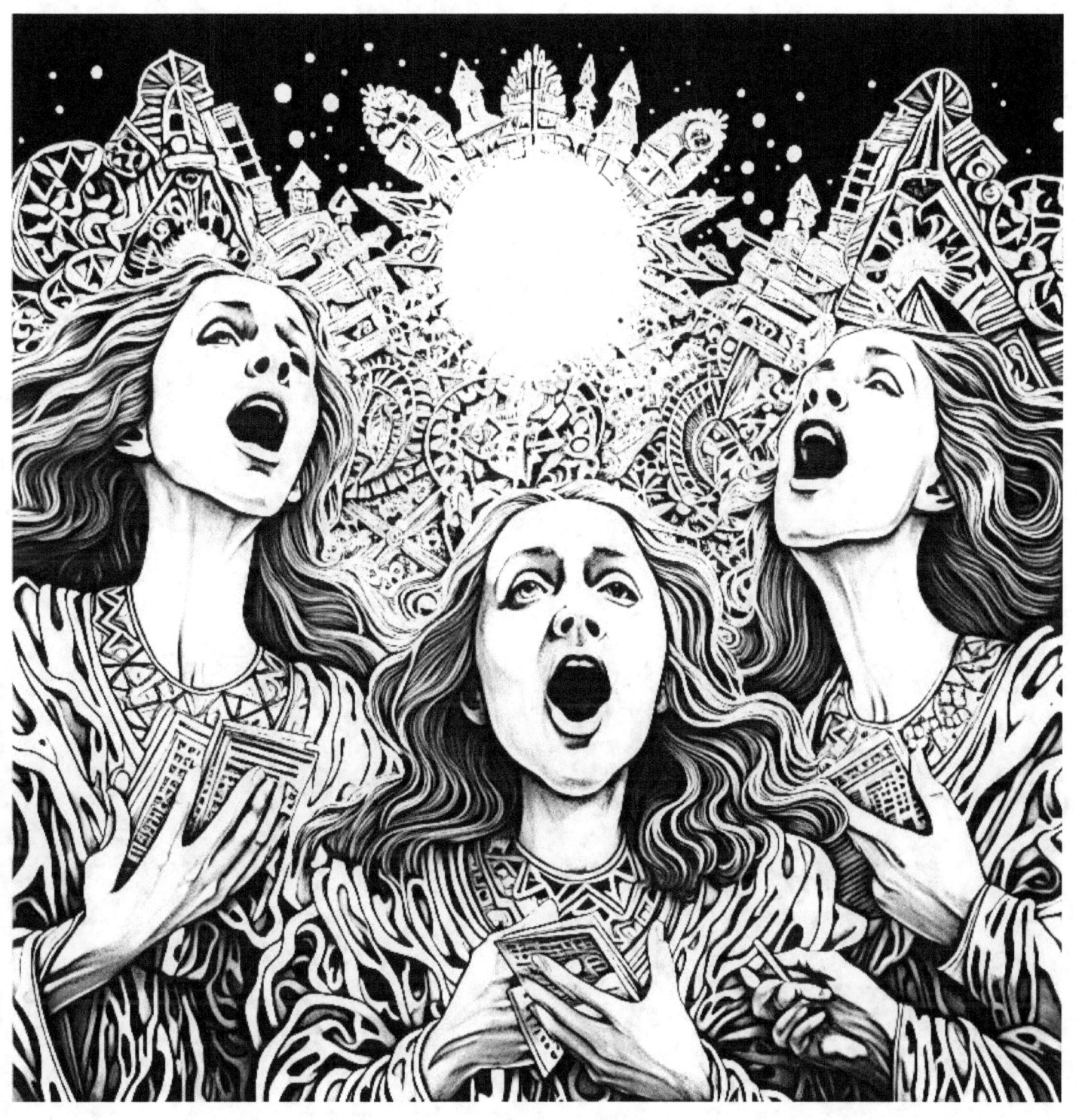

Exodus 23:20

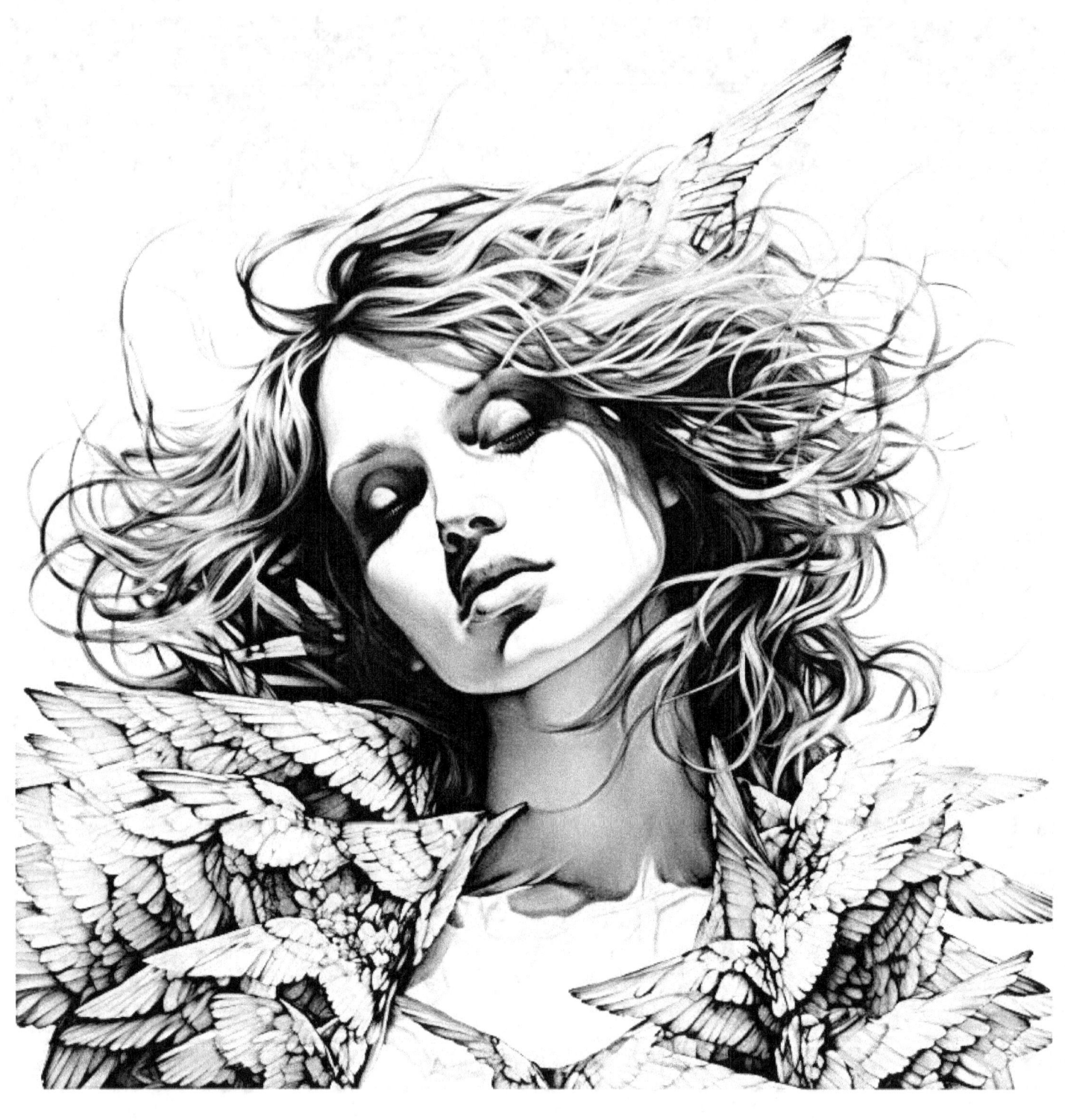

Hebrews 13:2

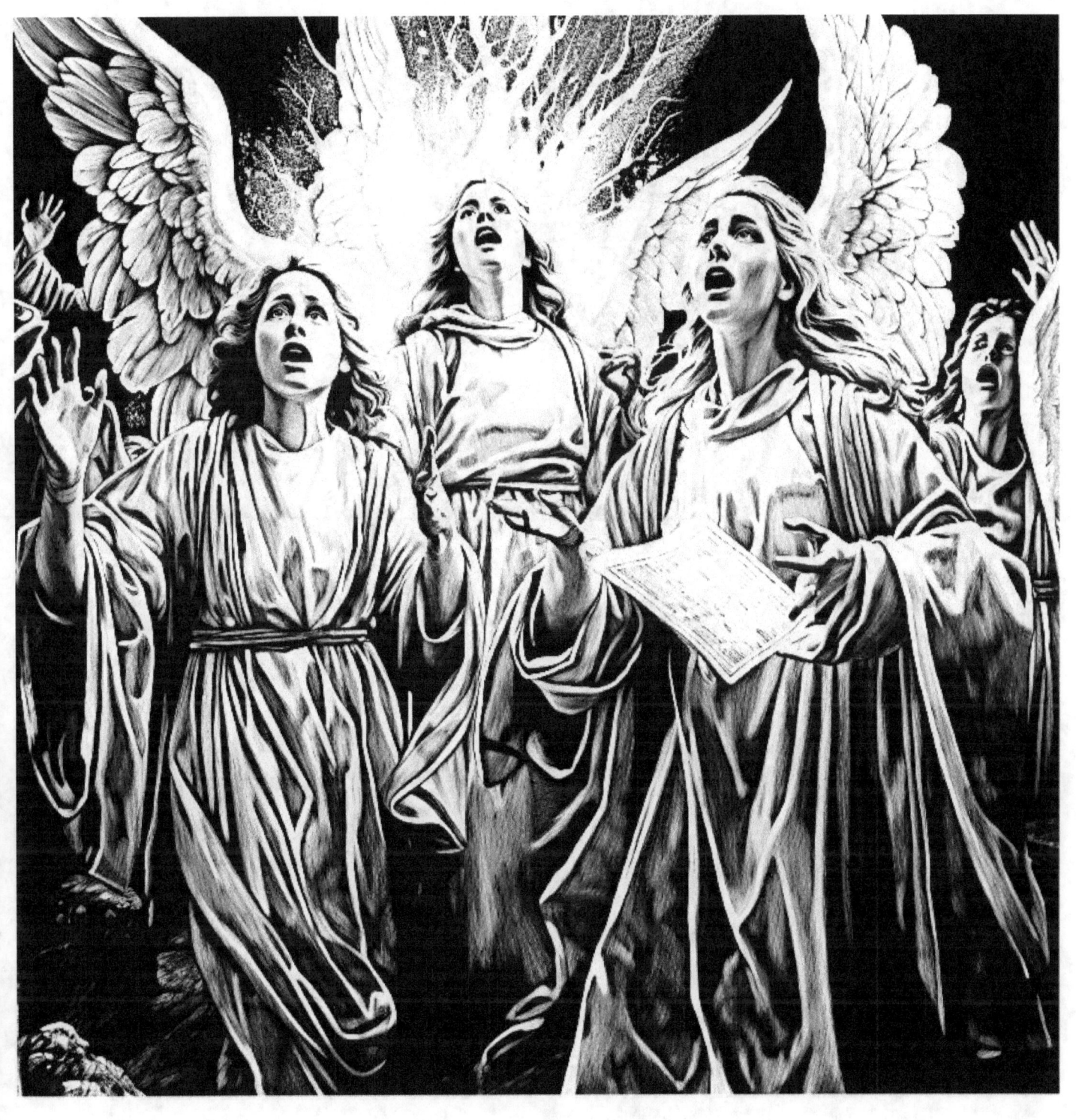

Hebrews 1:14

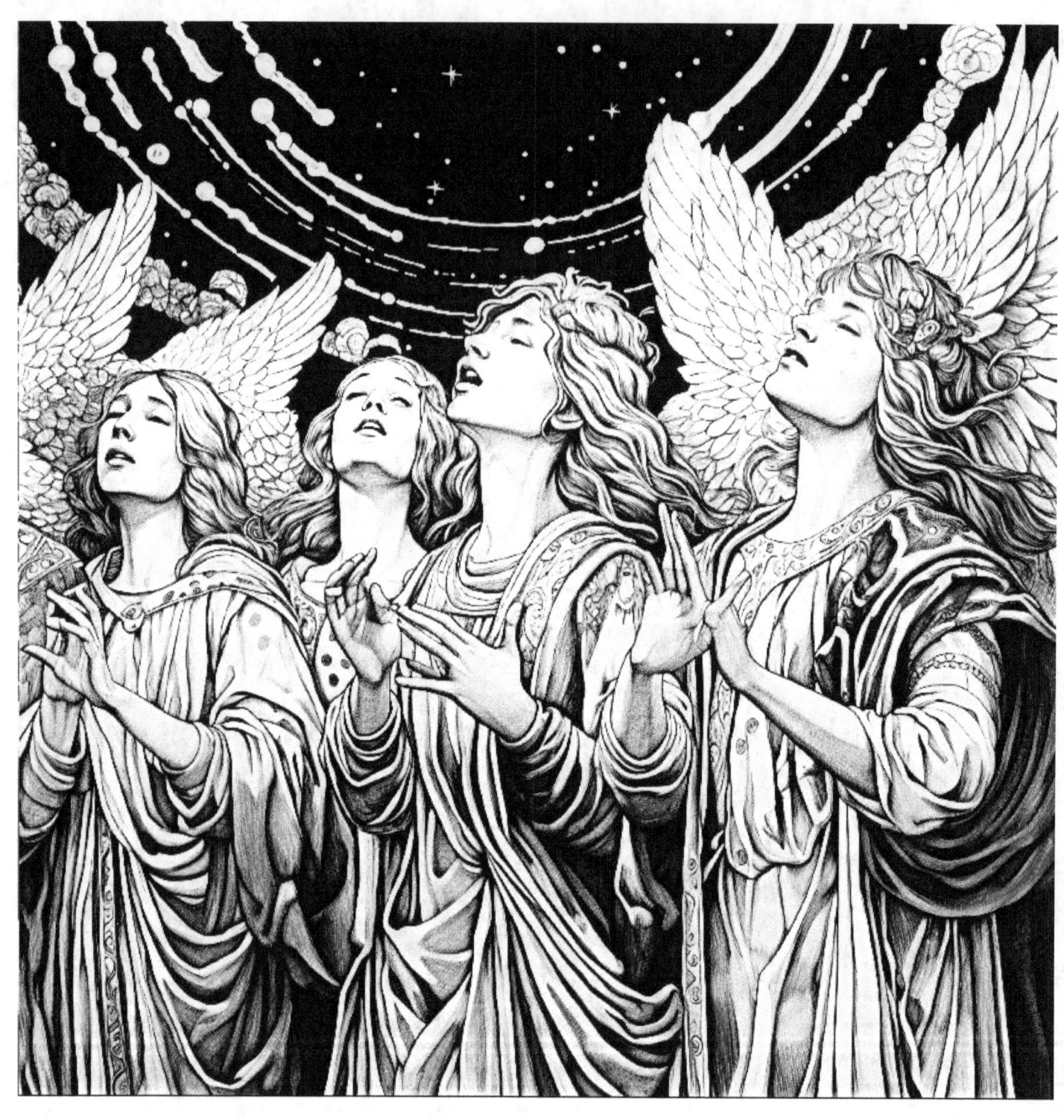

acts 8:26

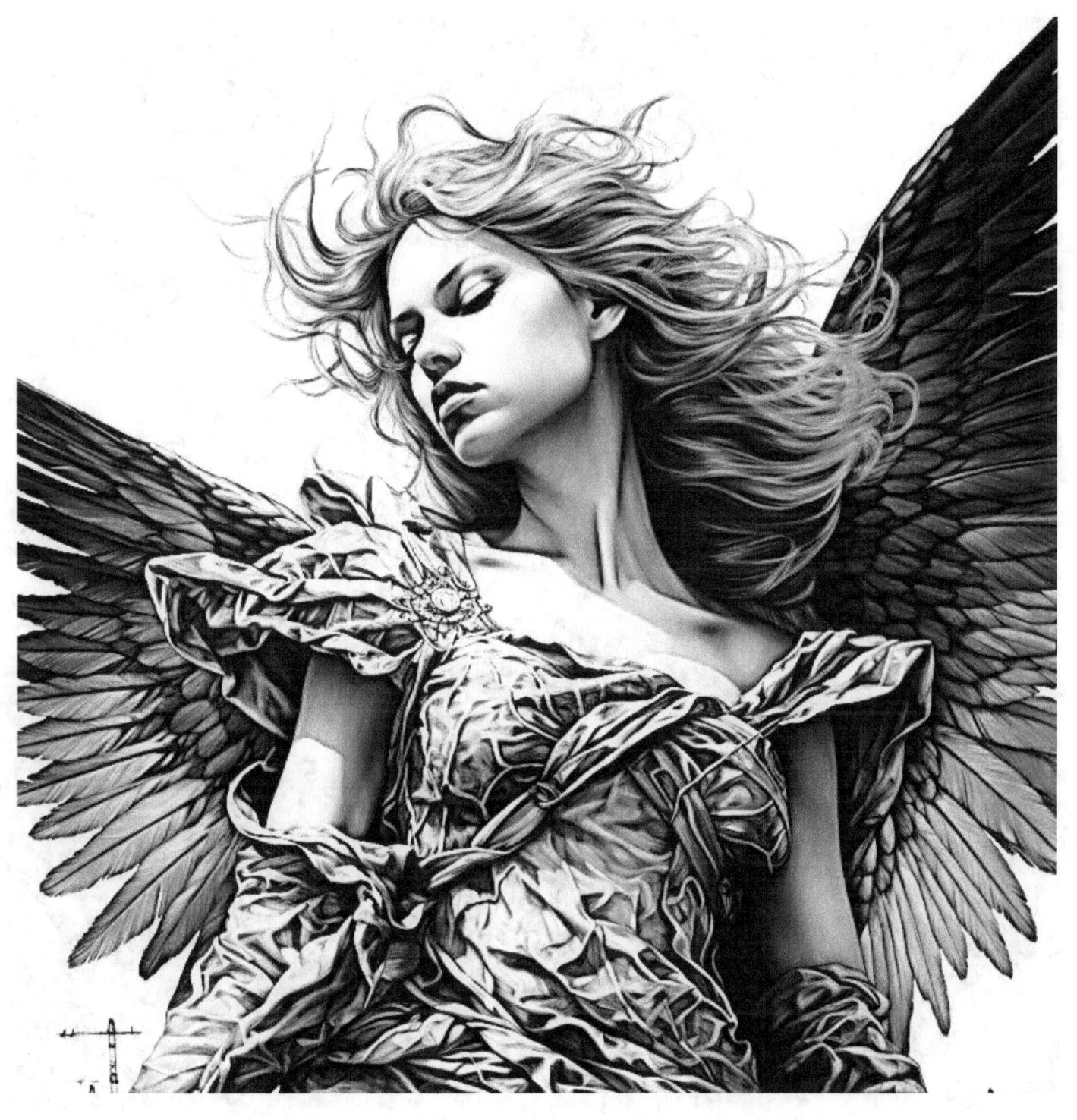

Luke 20:36

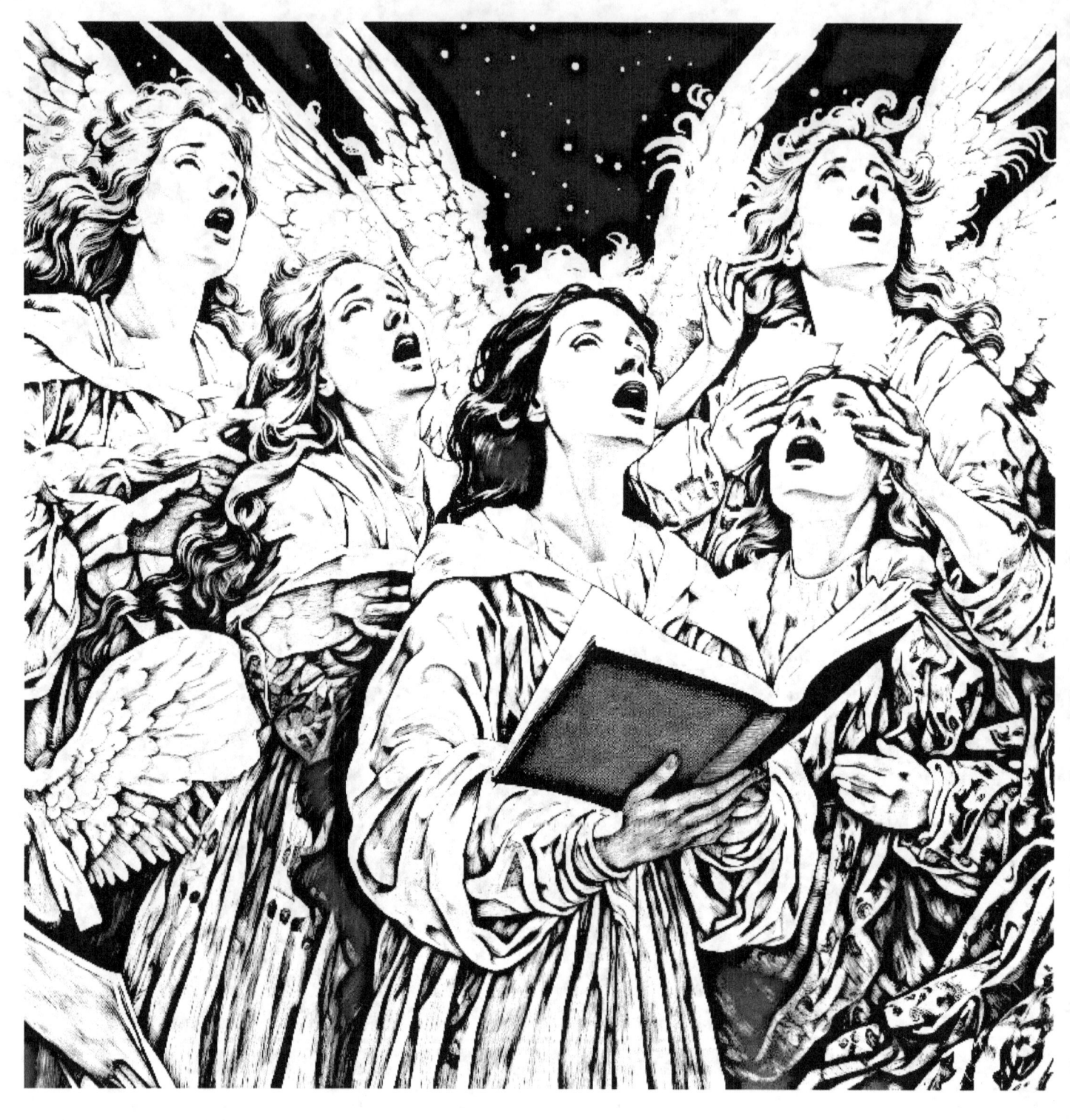

2 Peter 2:11

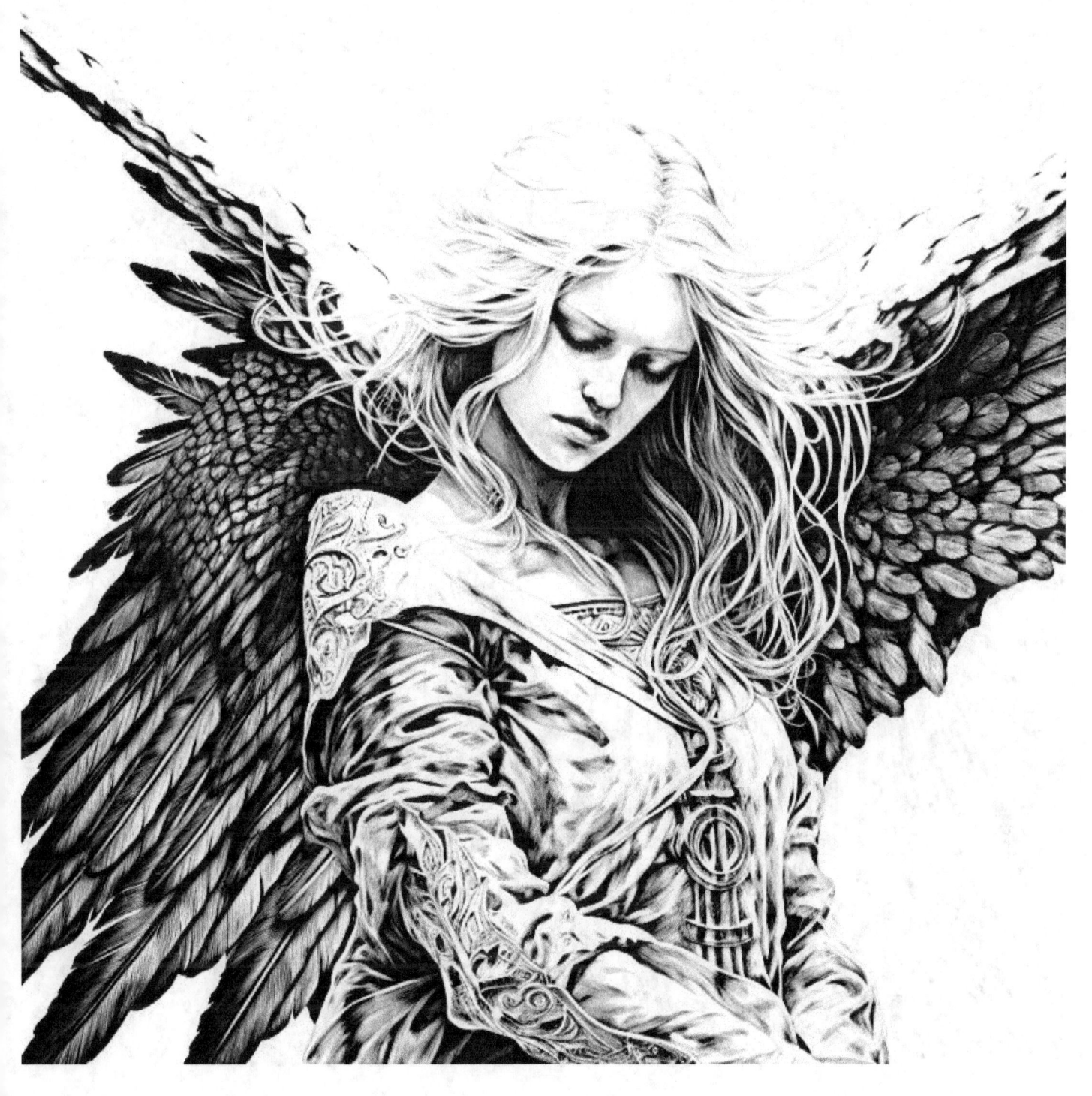

acts 7:53

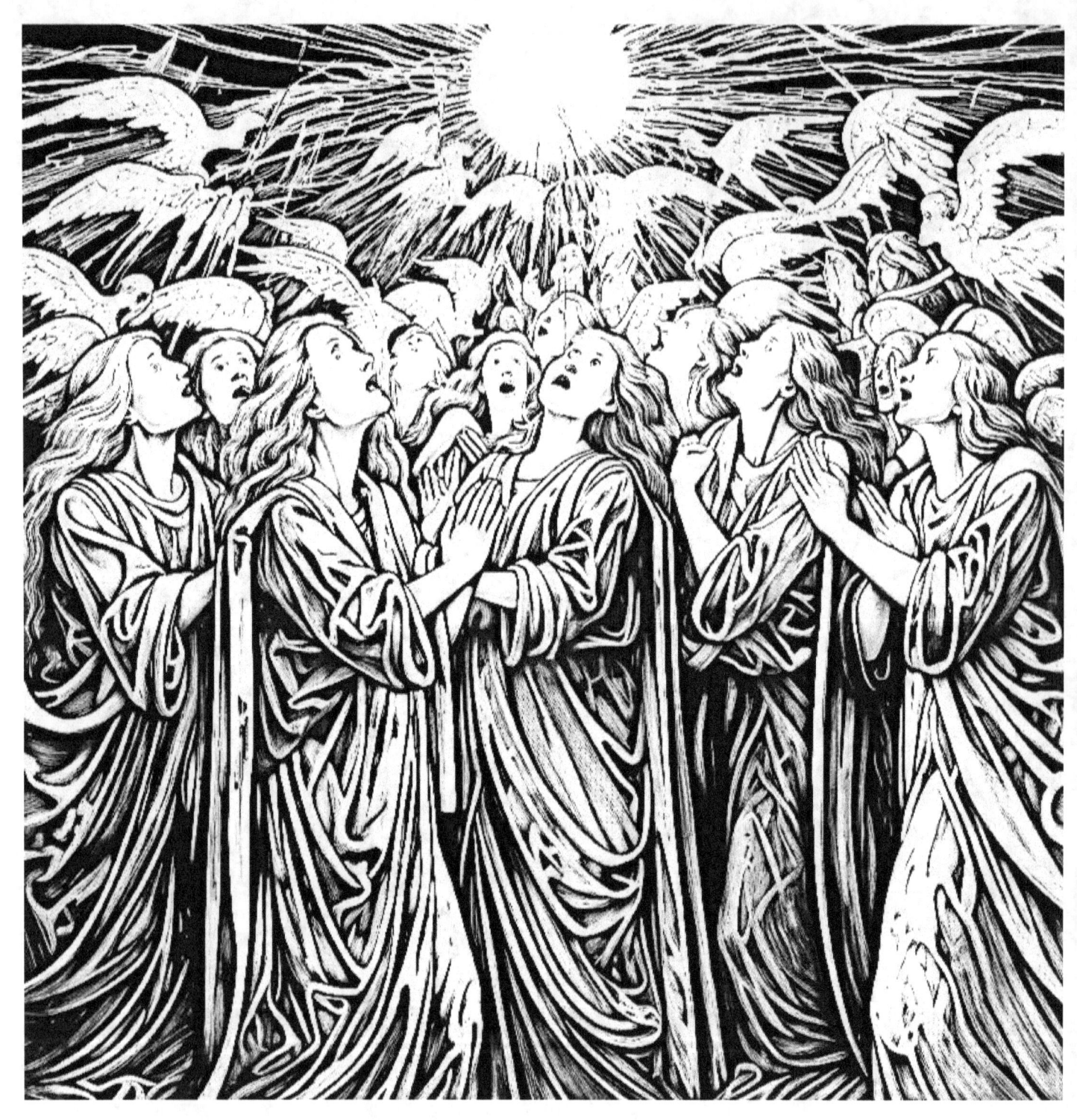

Hebrews 1:6

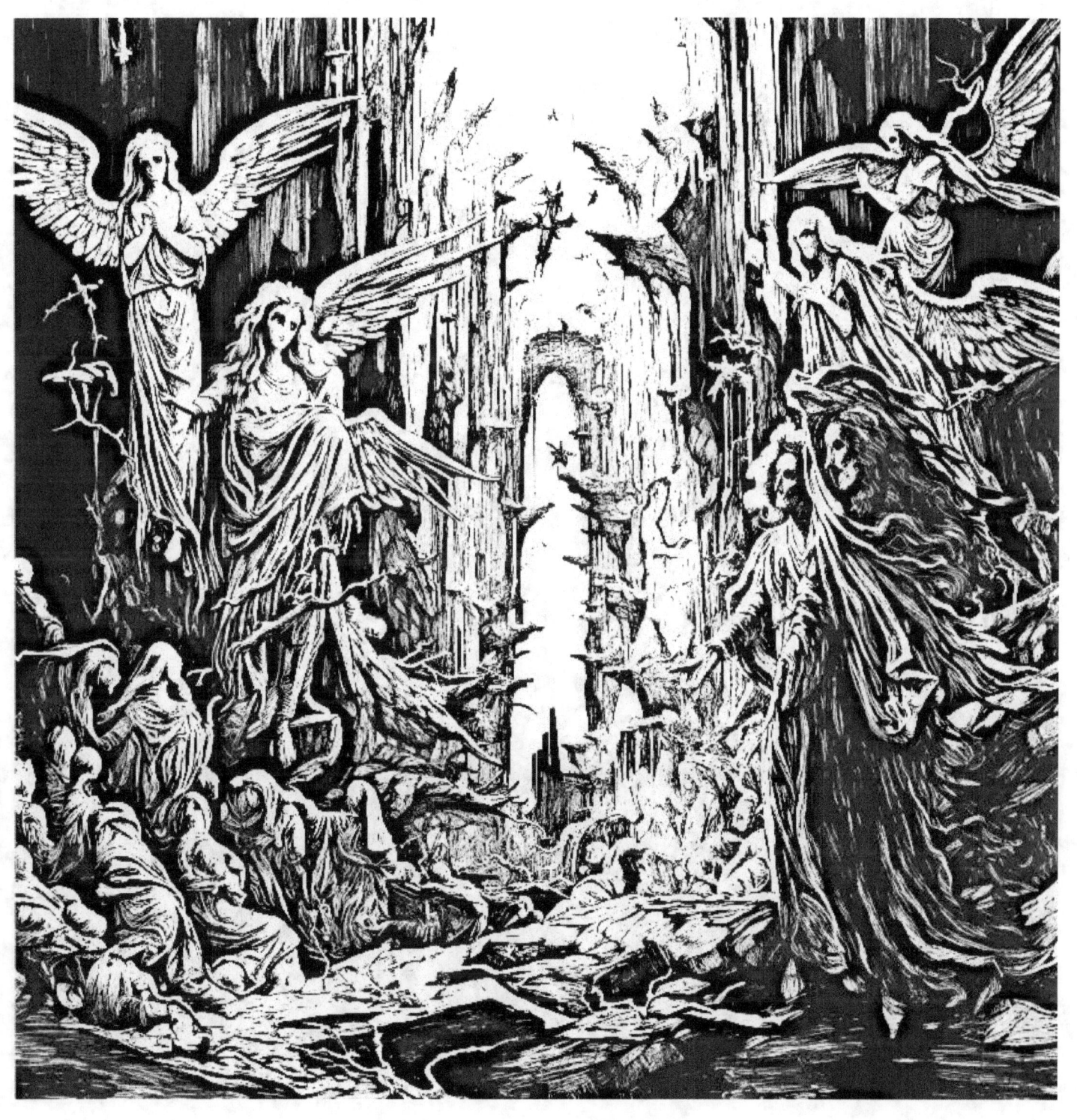

Exodus 25:20

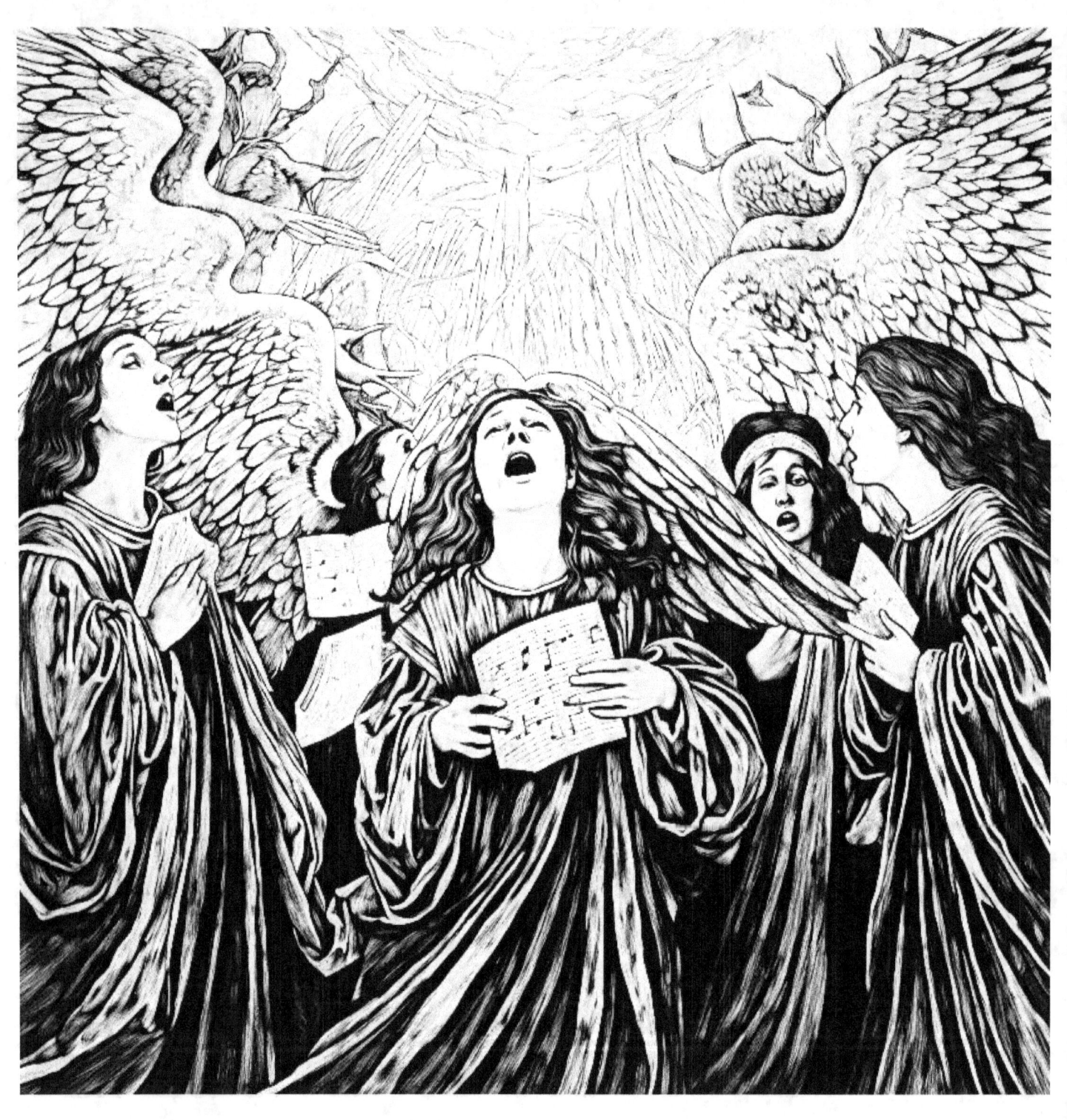

2 Thessalonians 1:7

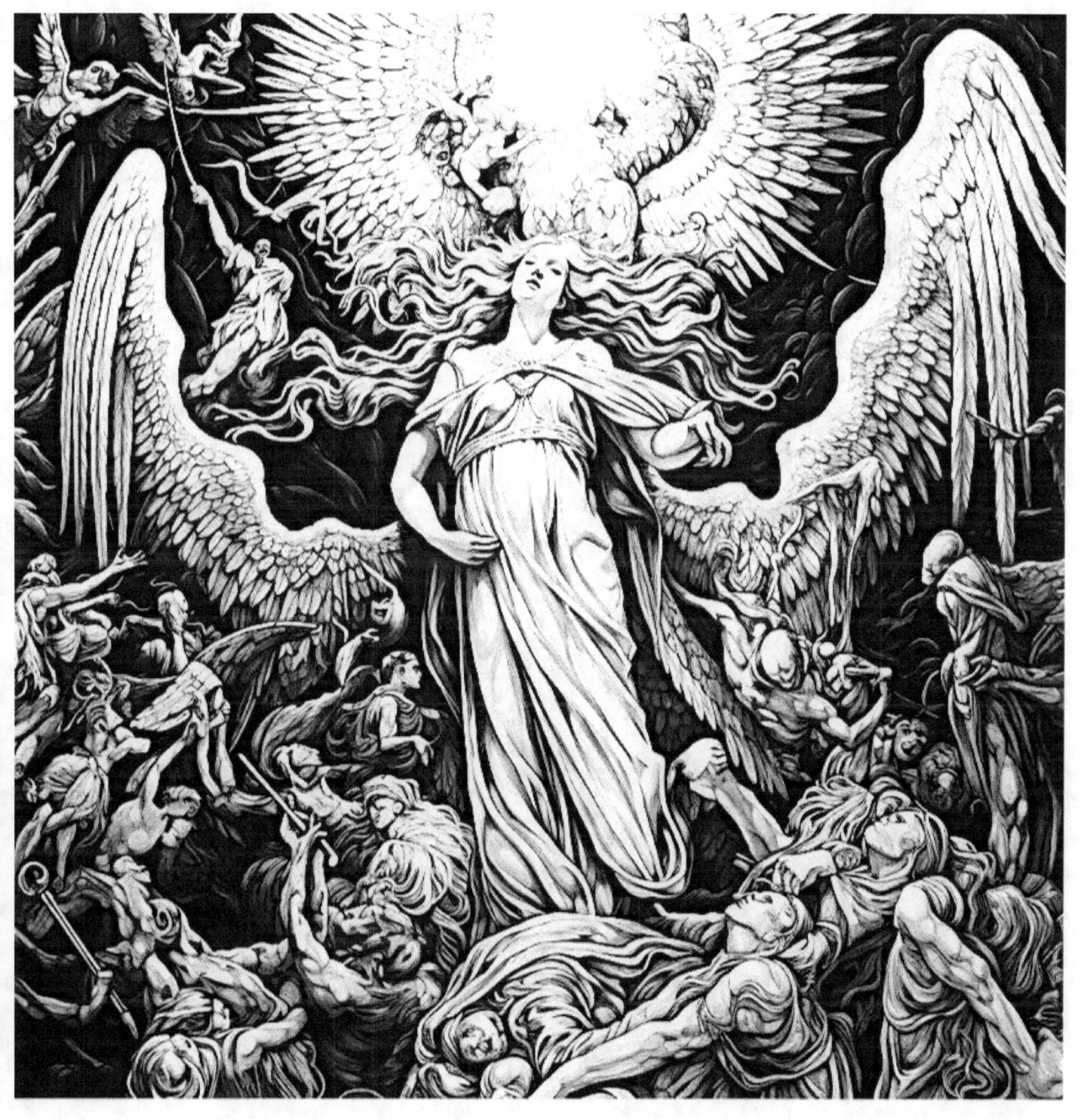

Luke 1:11-13

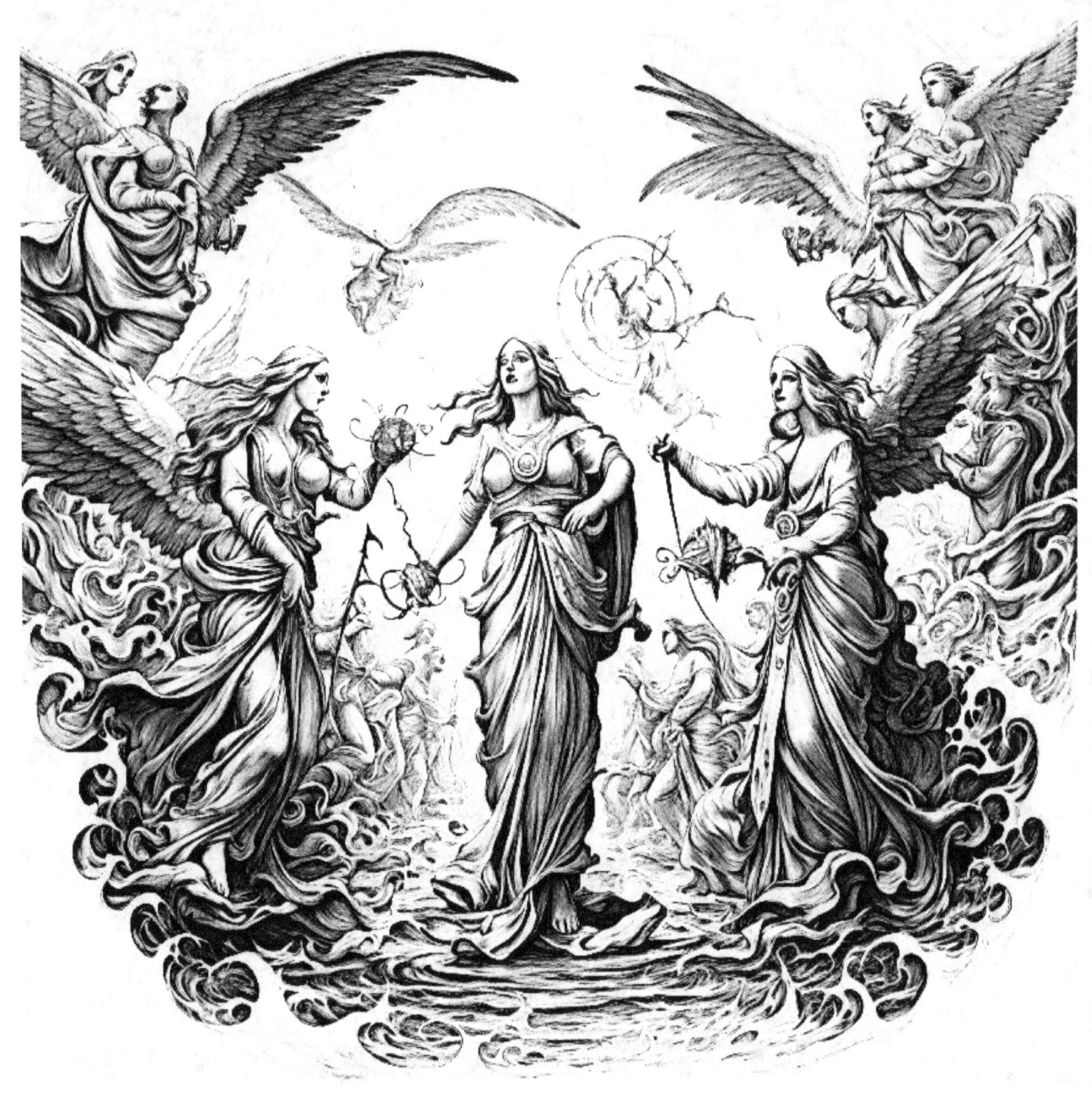

acts 27:23

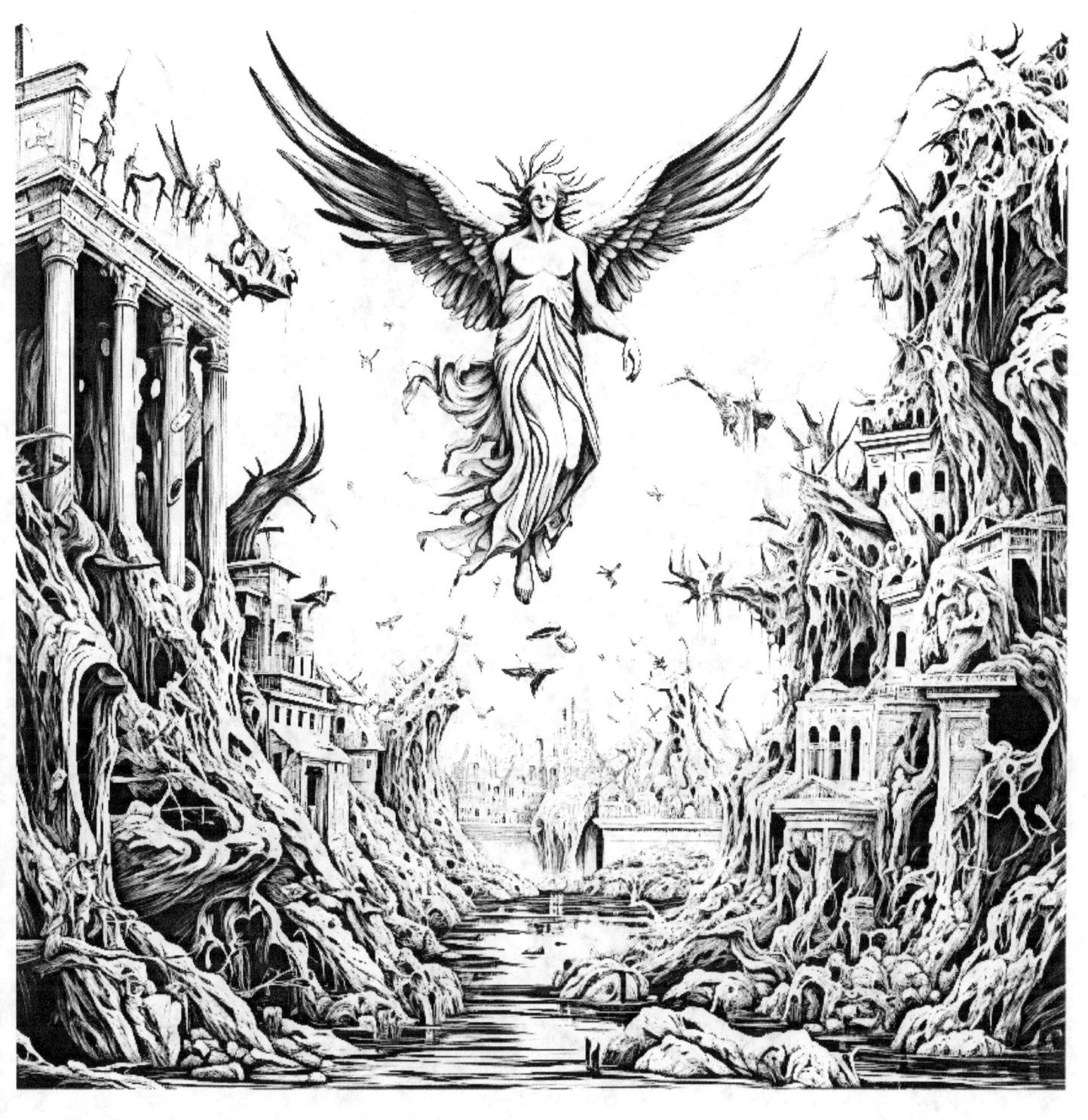

1 Thessalonians 4:16-1

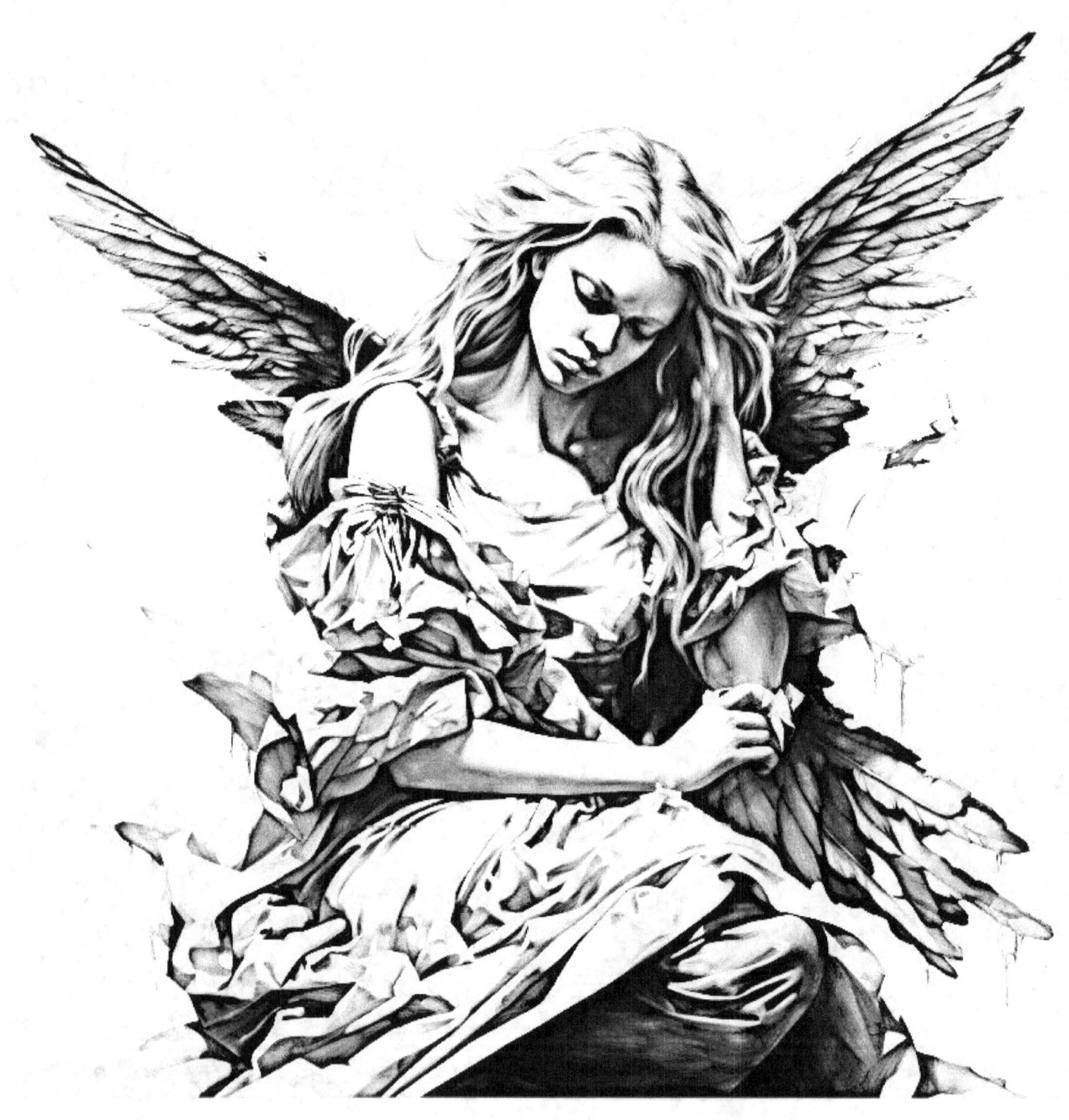

Matthew 18:10

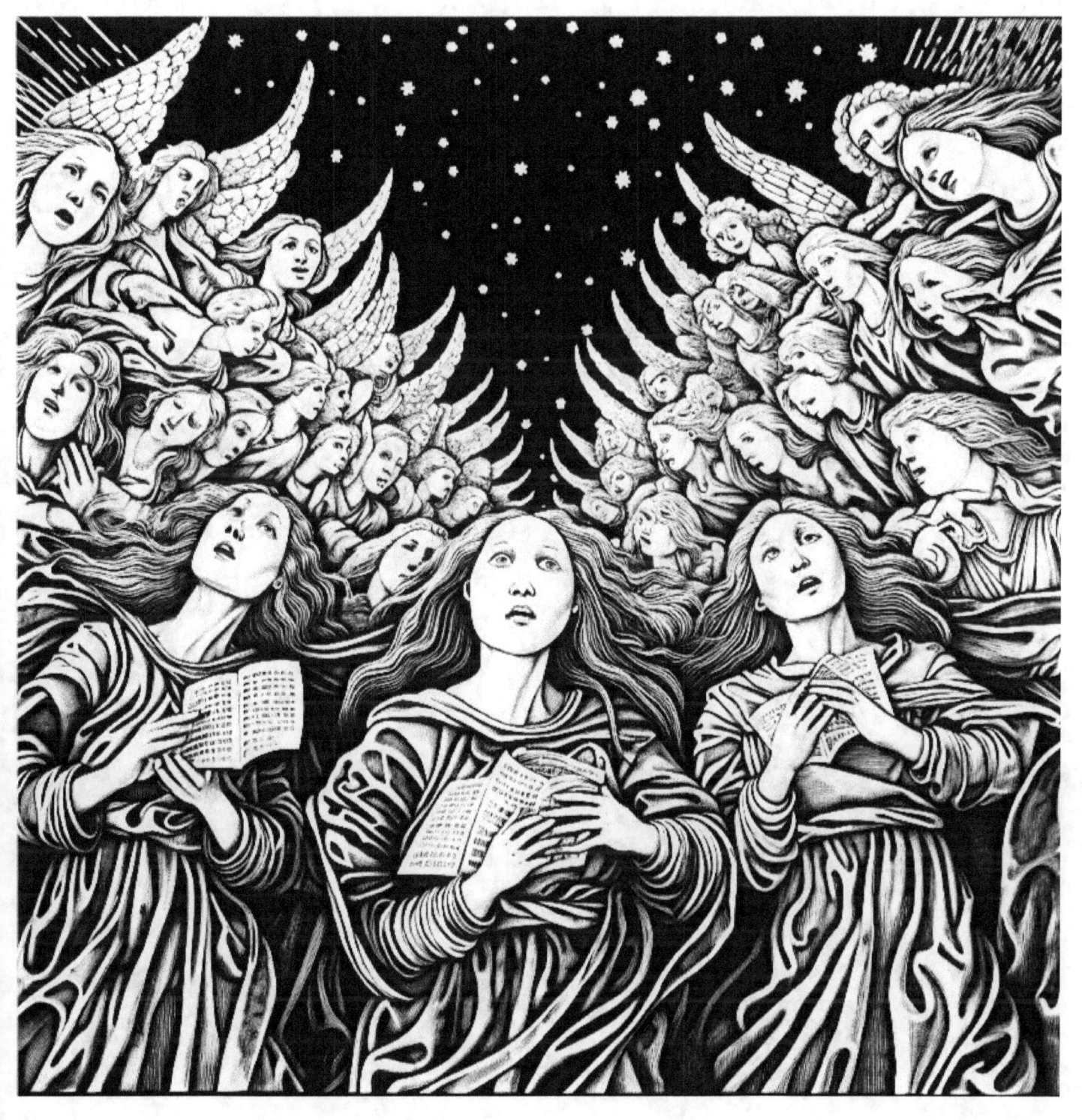

Matthew 16:27

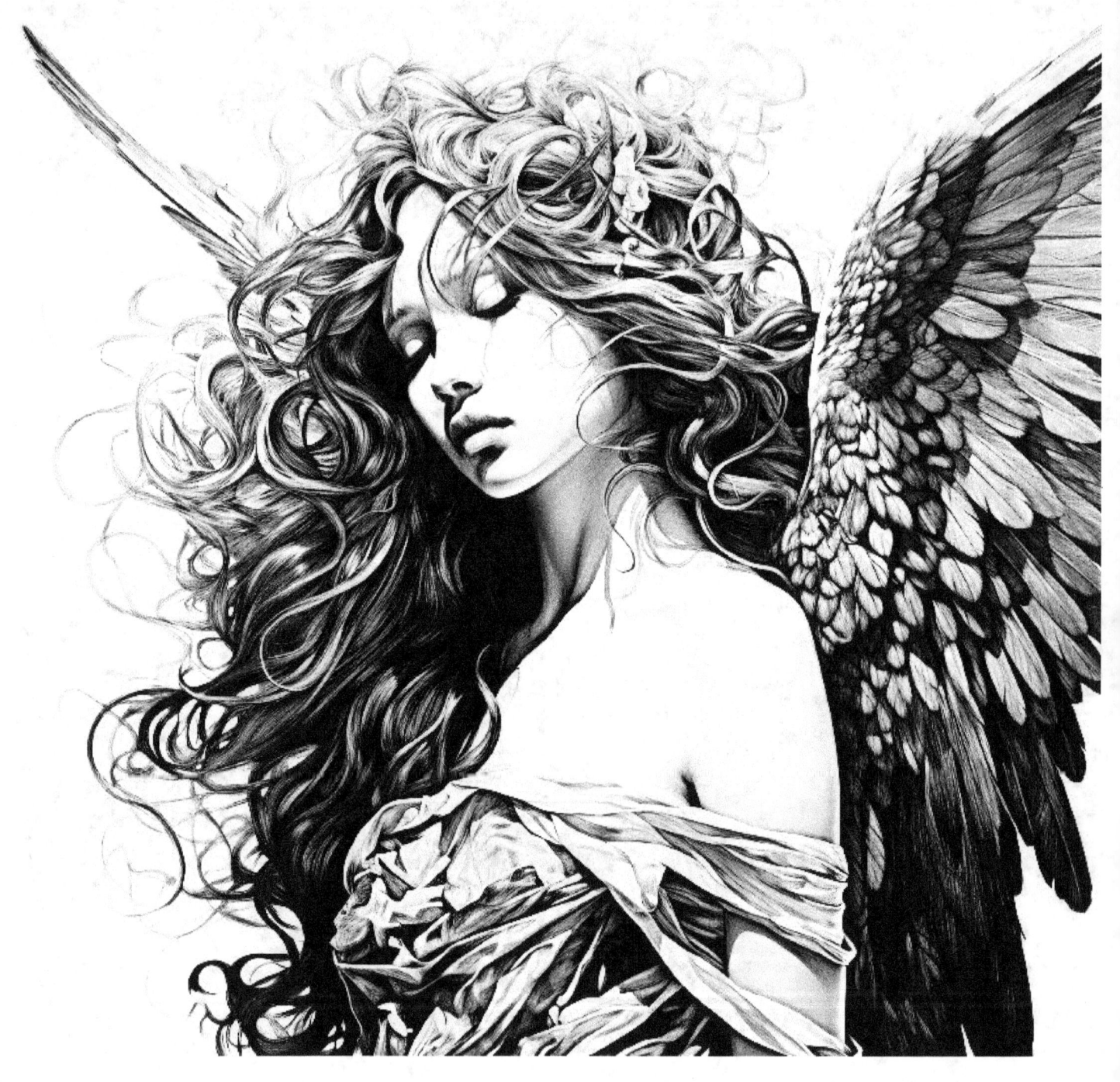

acts 5:19

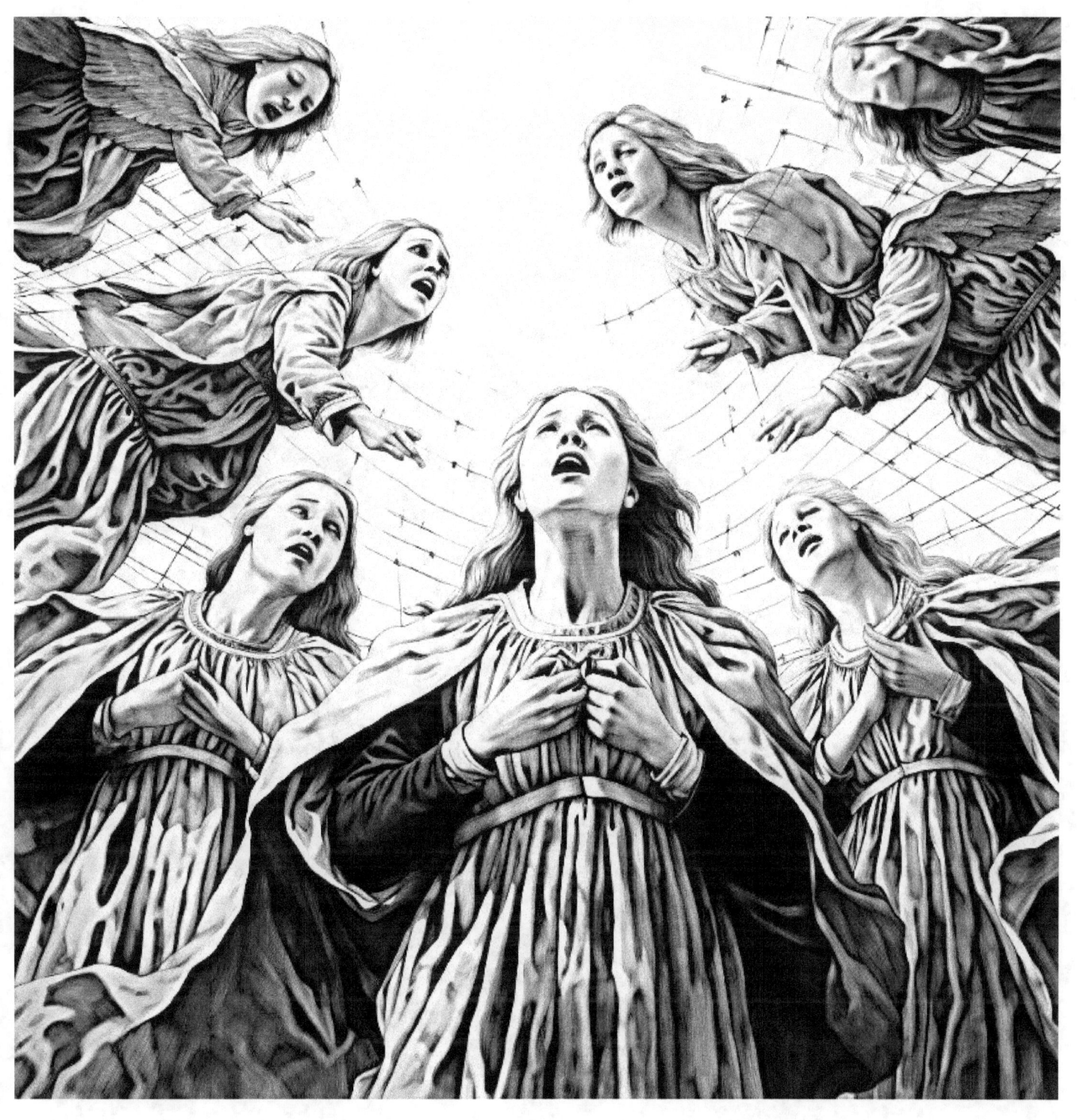

Mark 8:38

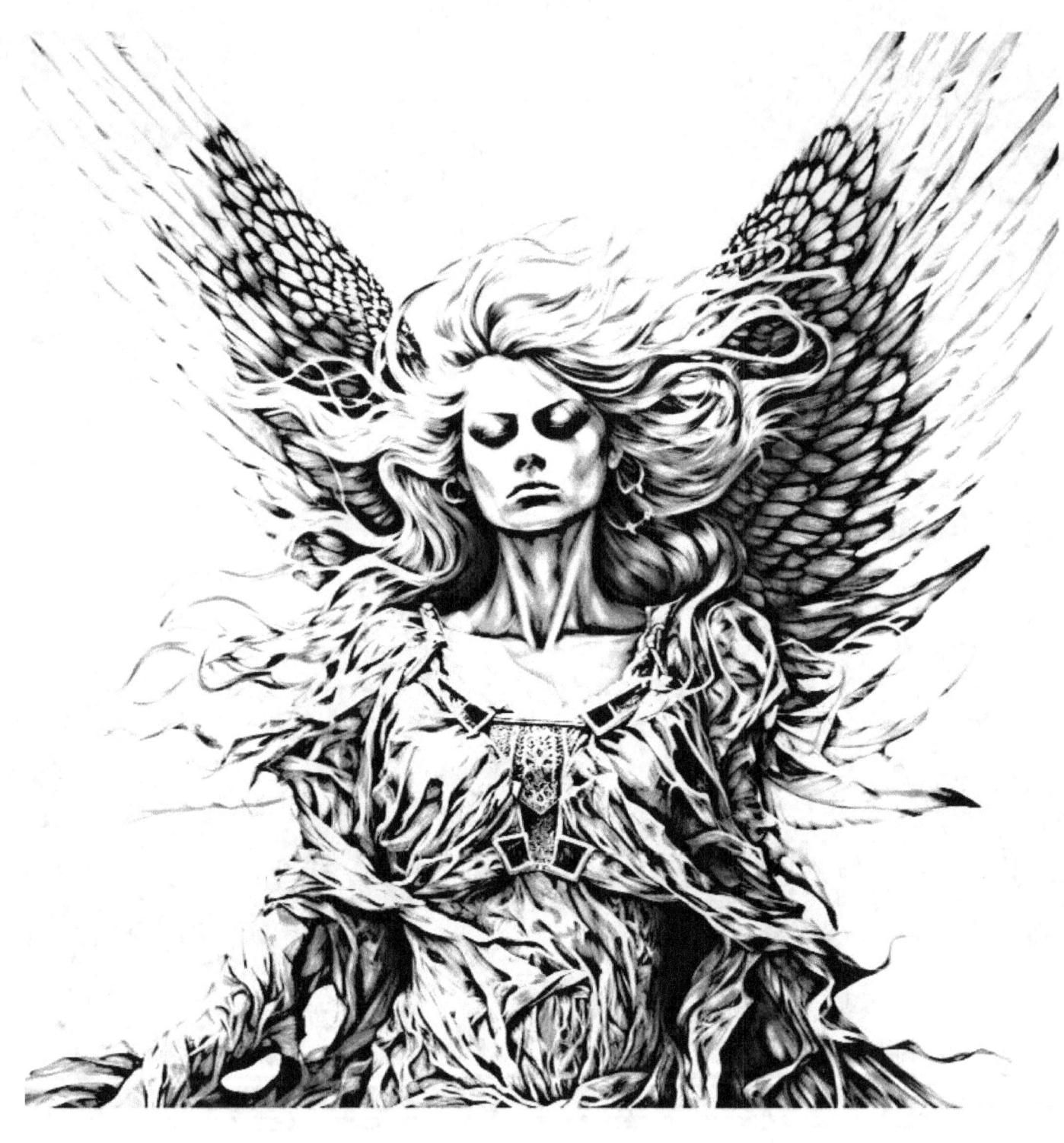

Revelation 1:1

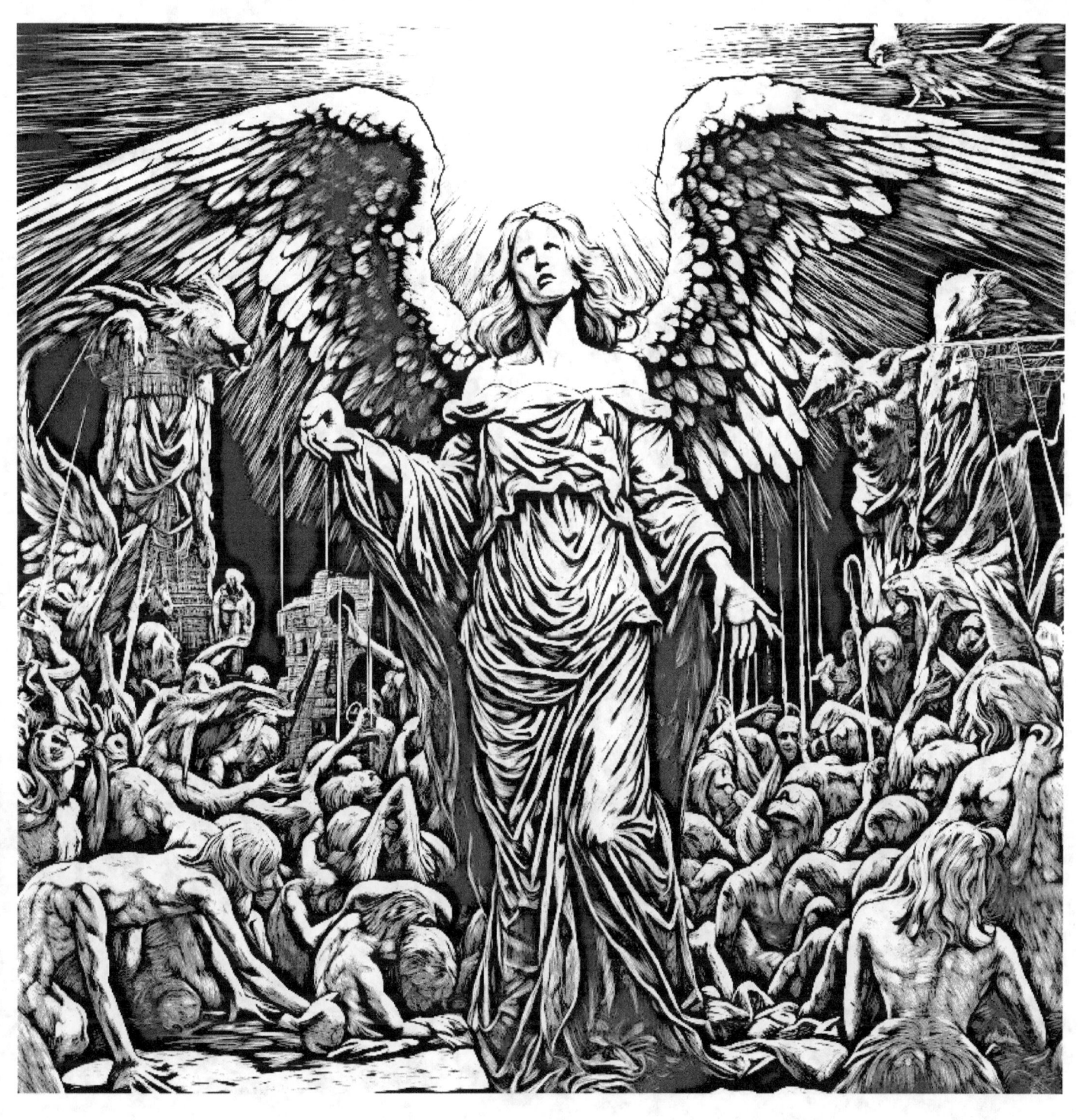

1 Thessalonians 4:16

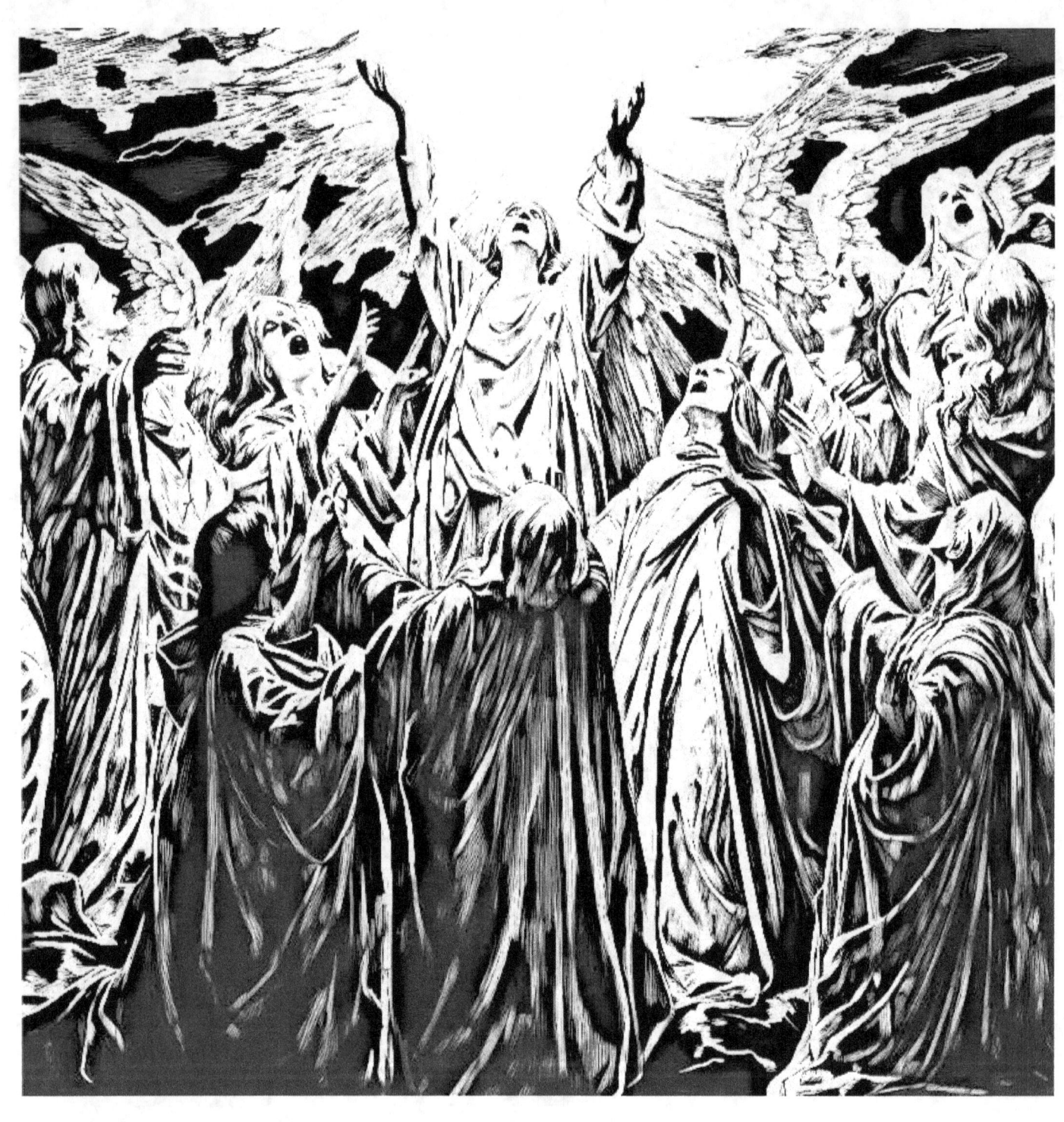

Luke 16:22

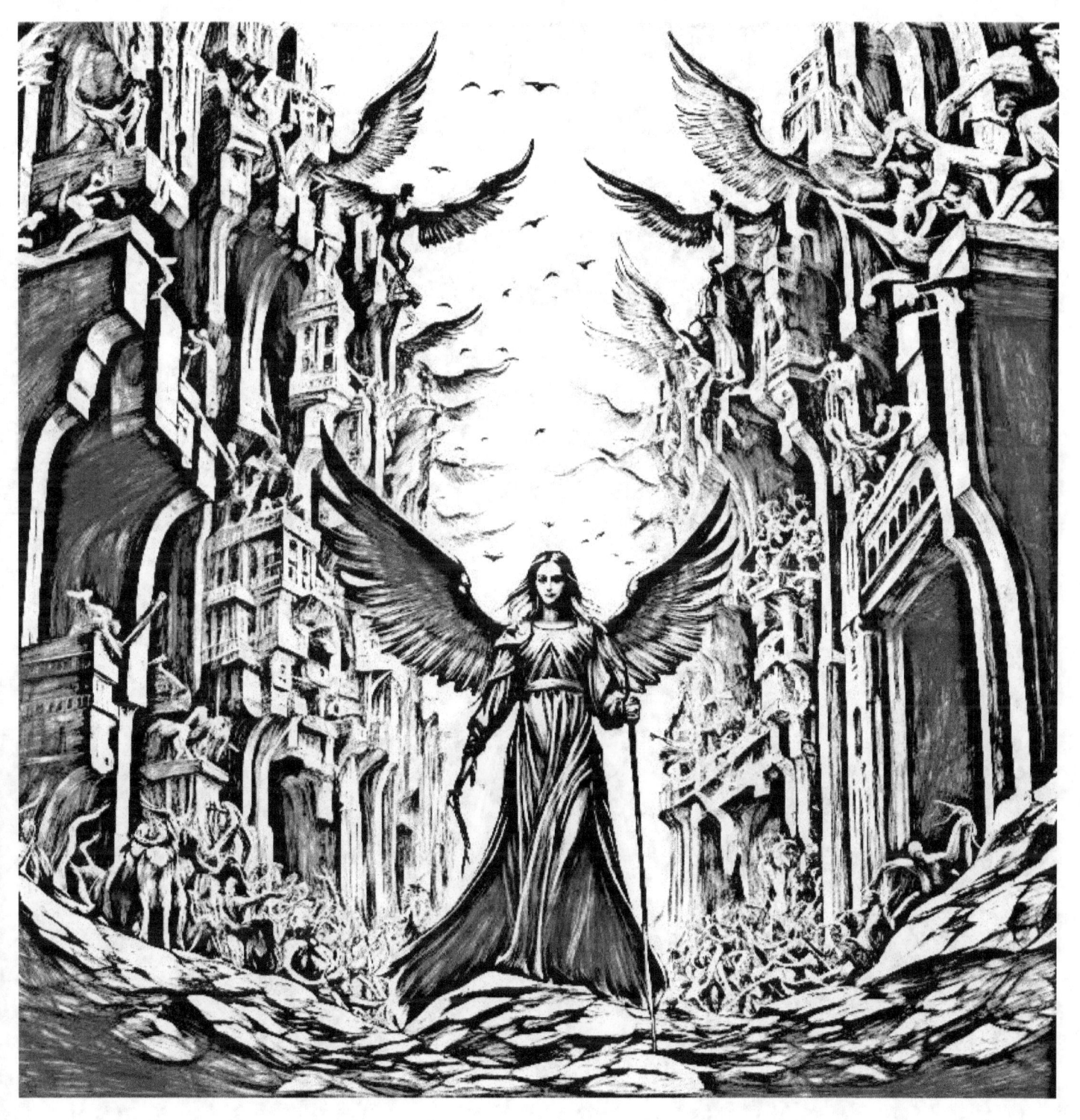

1 Timothy 3:16

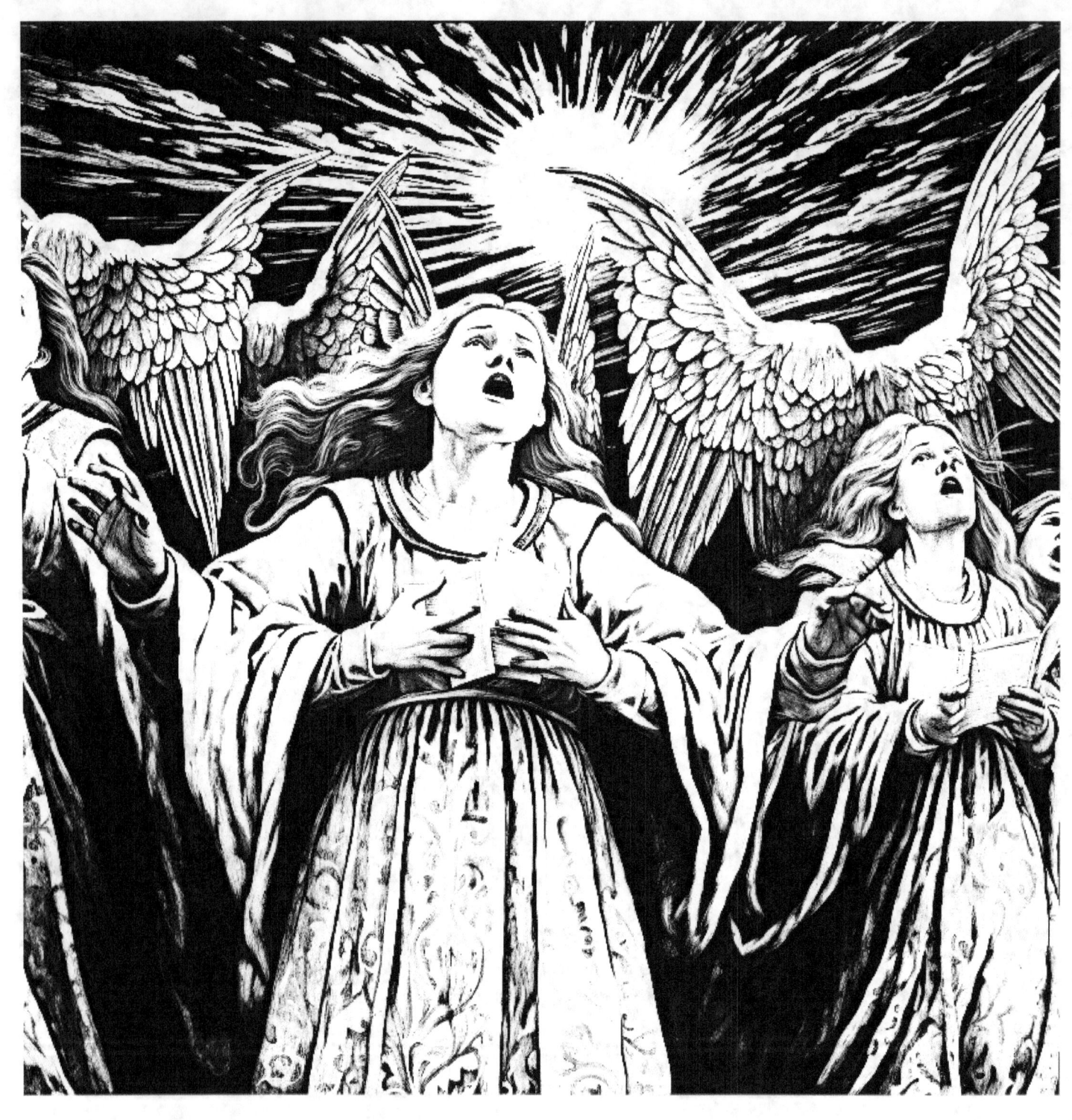

Matthew 13:49

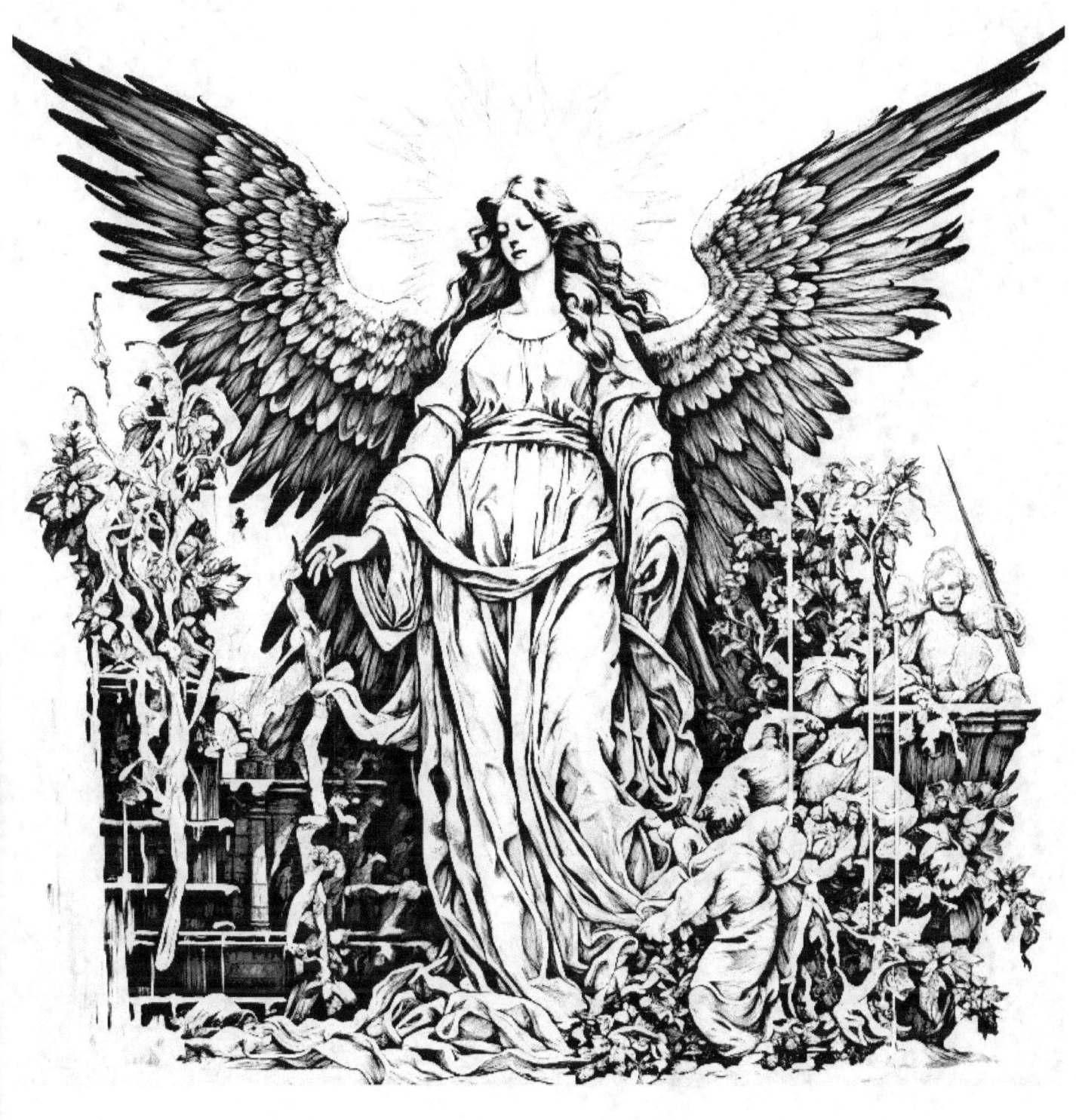

2 Kings 19:35

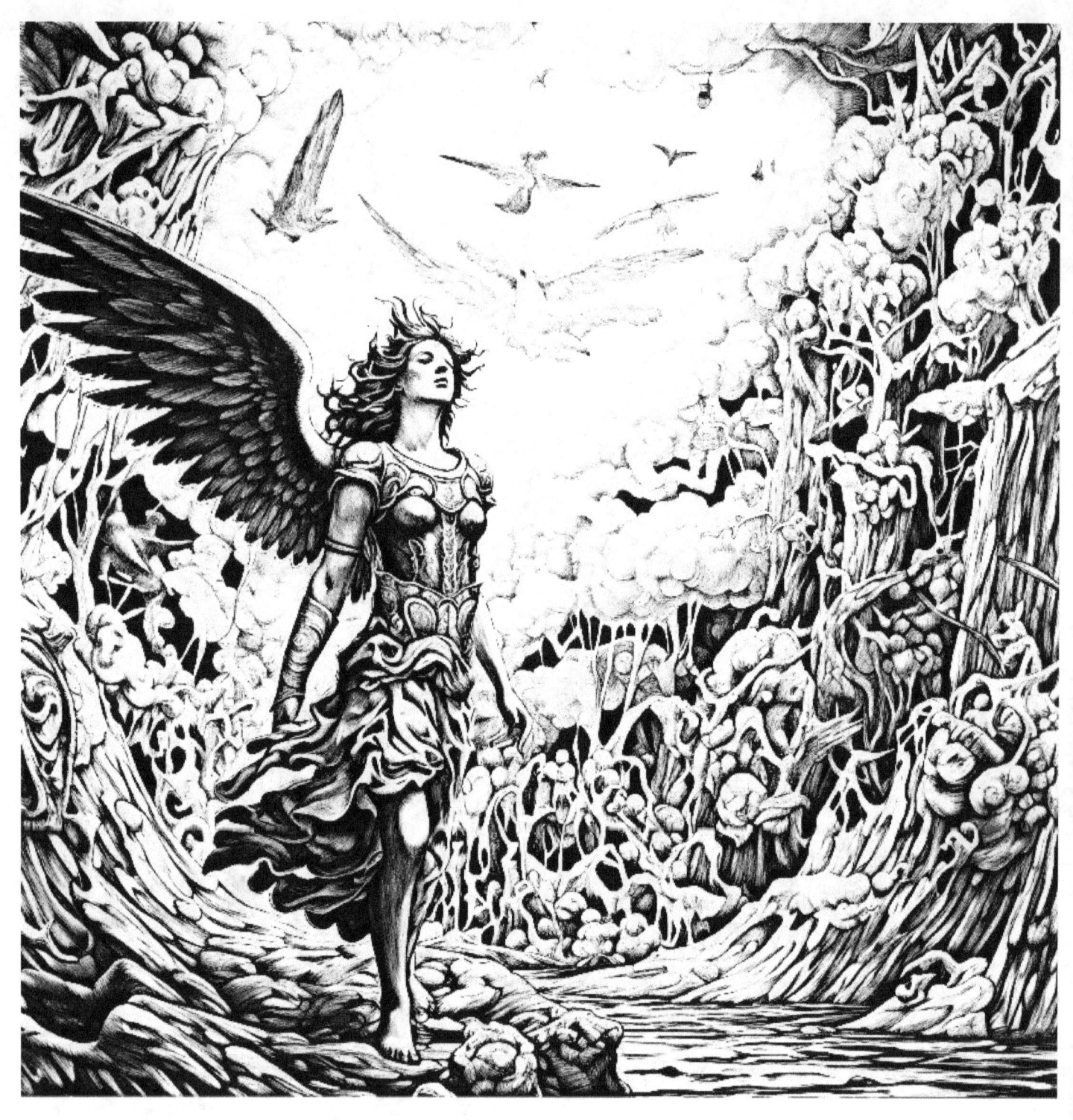

Matthew 4:6

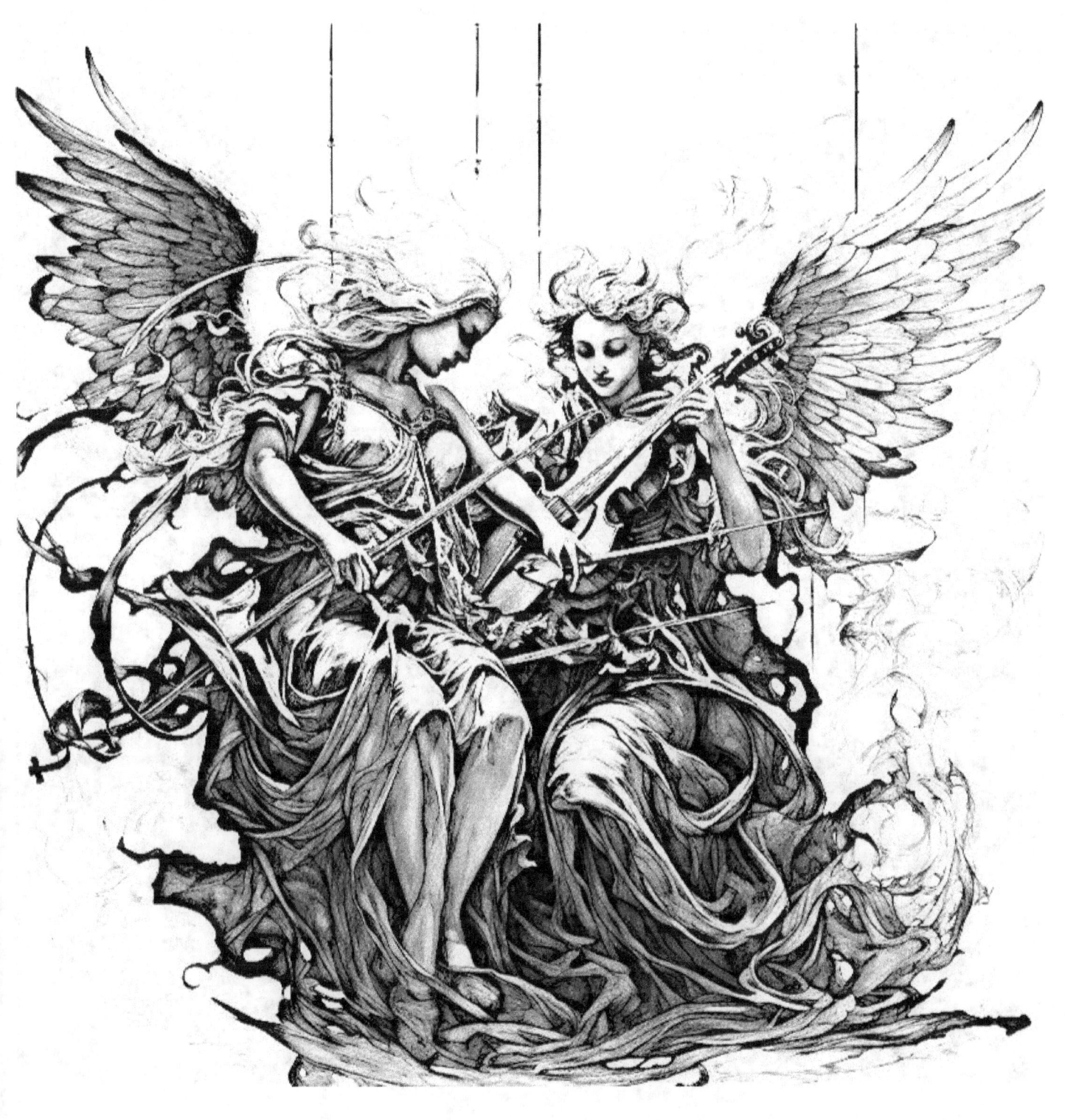

John 20:12

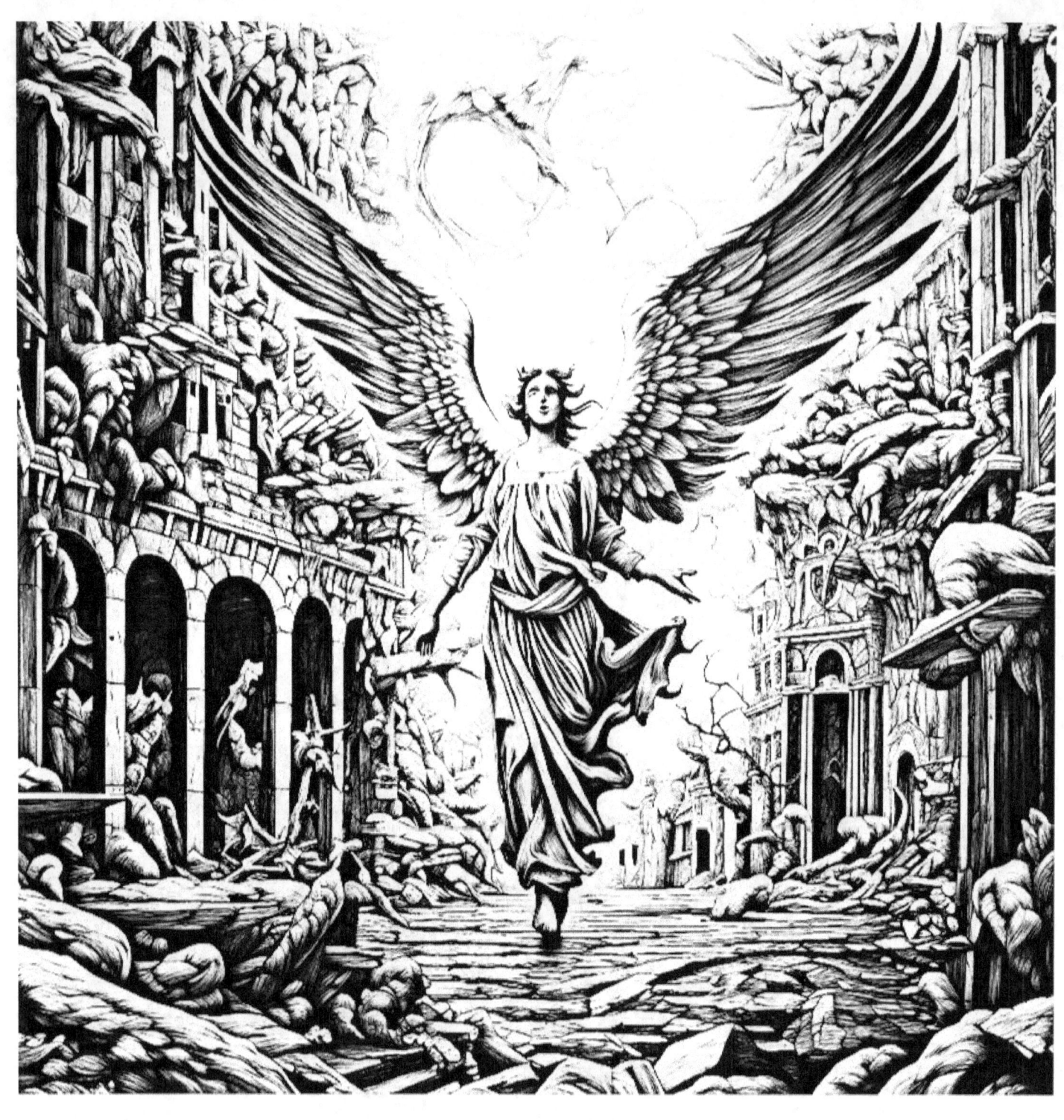

Judges 13:6

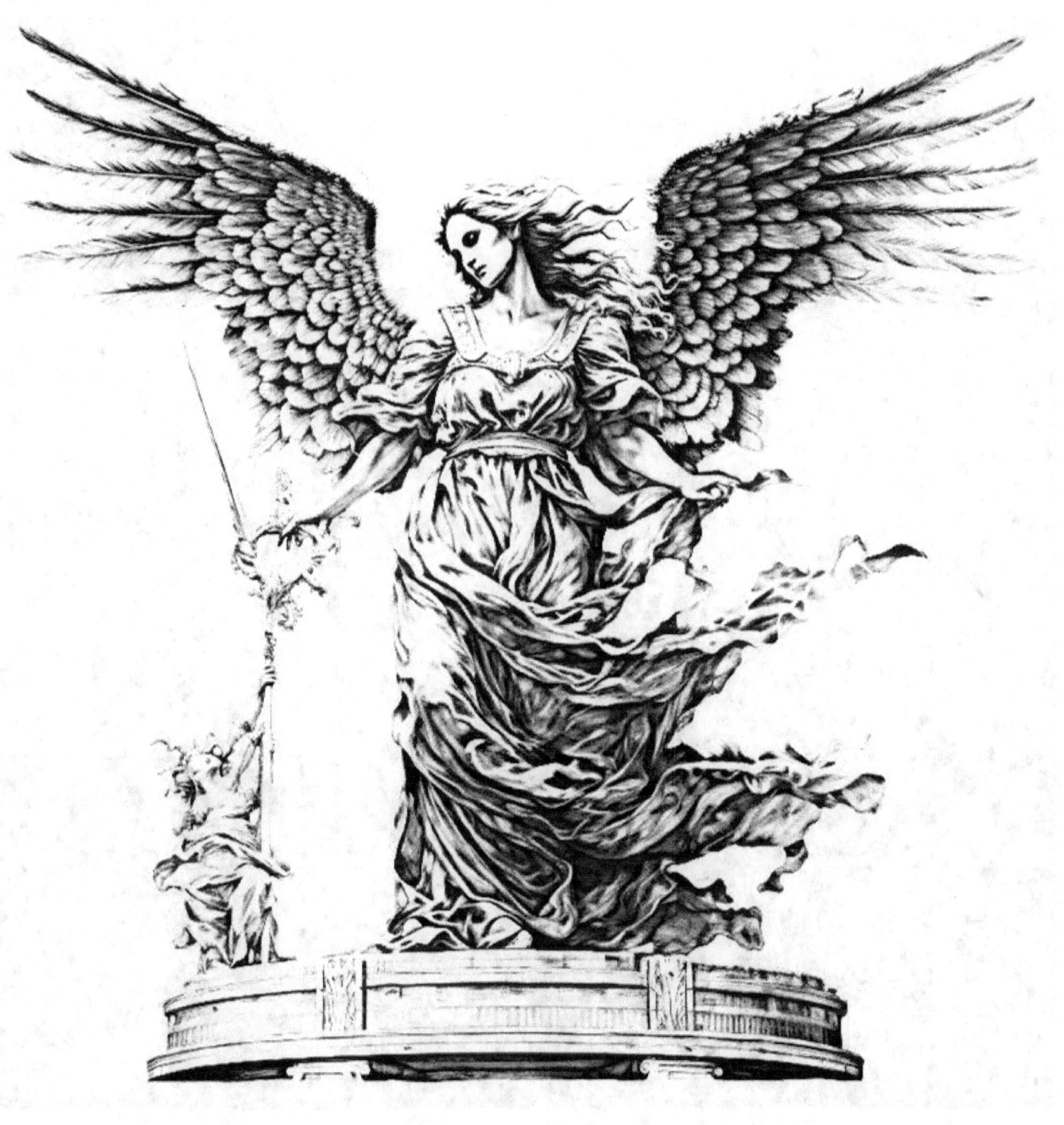

Luke 15:10

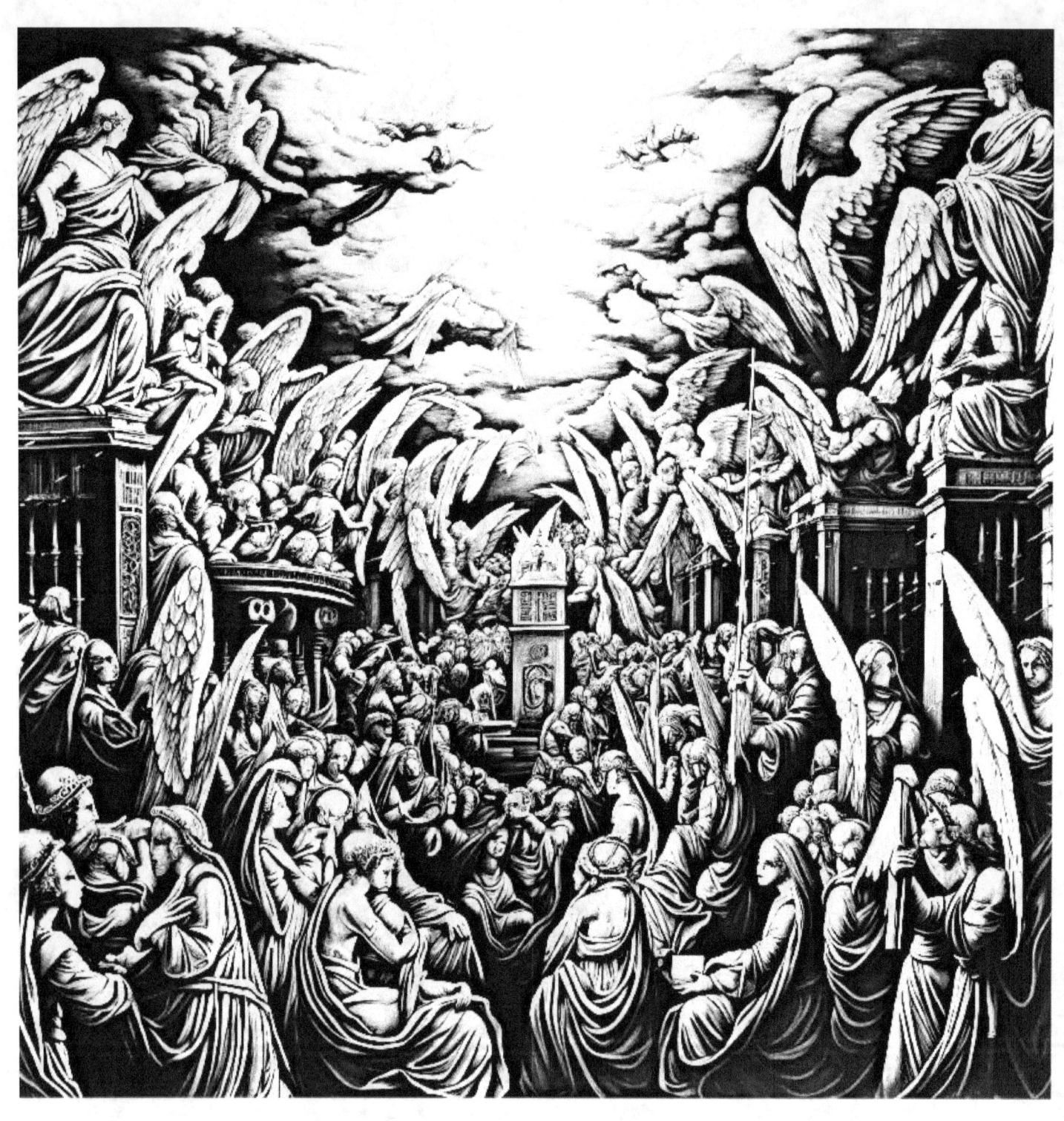

Hebrews 12:22

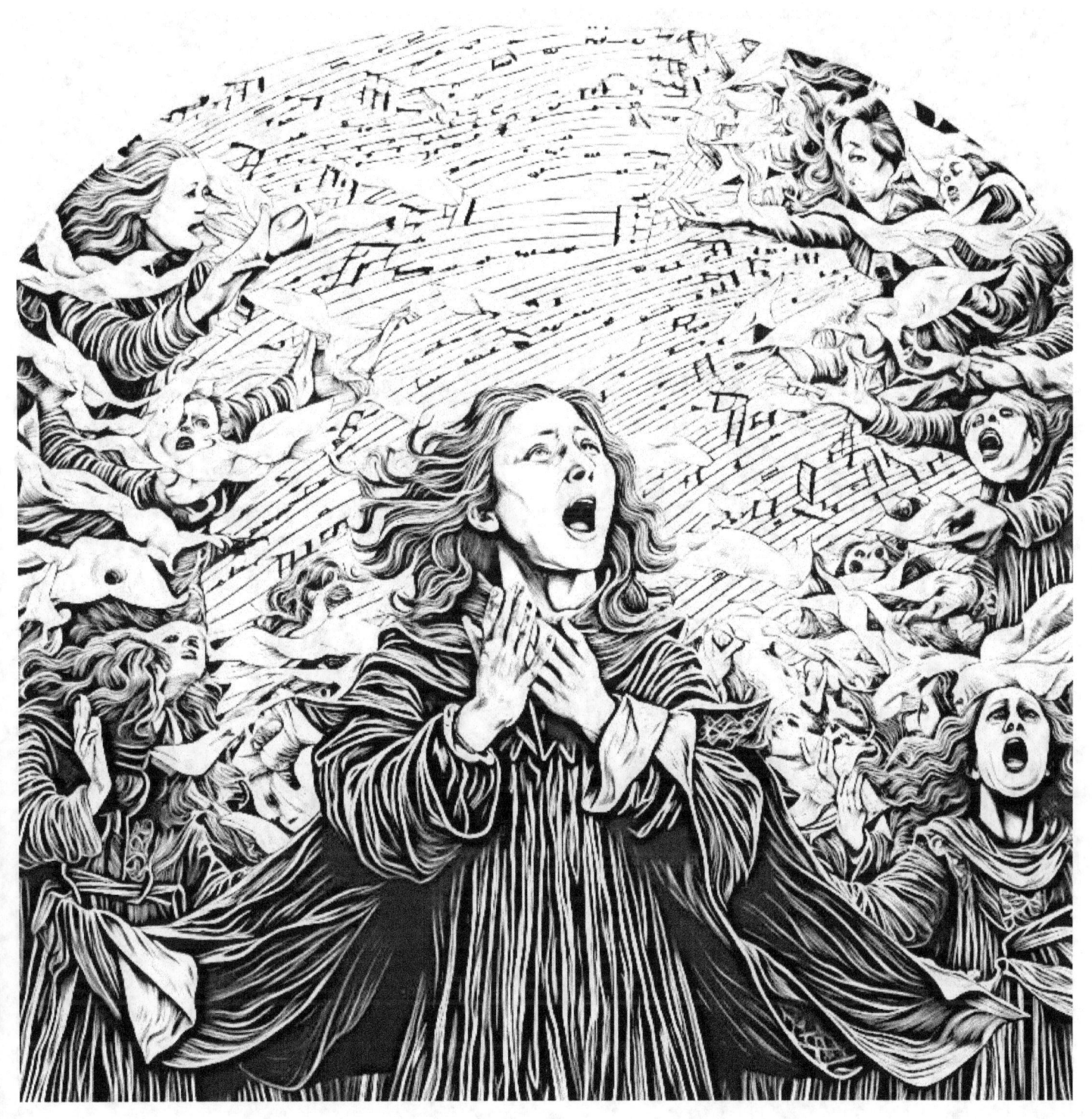

2 Samuel 24:16

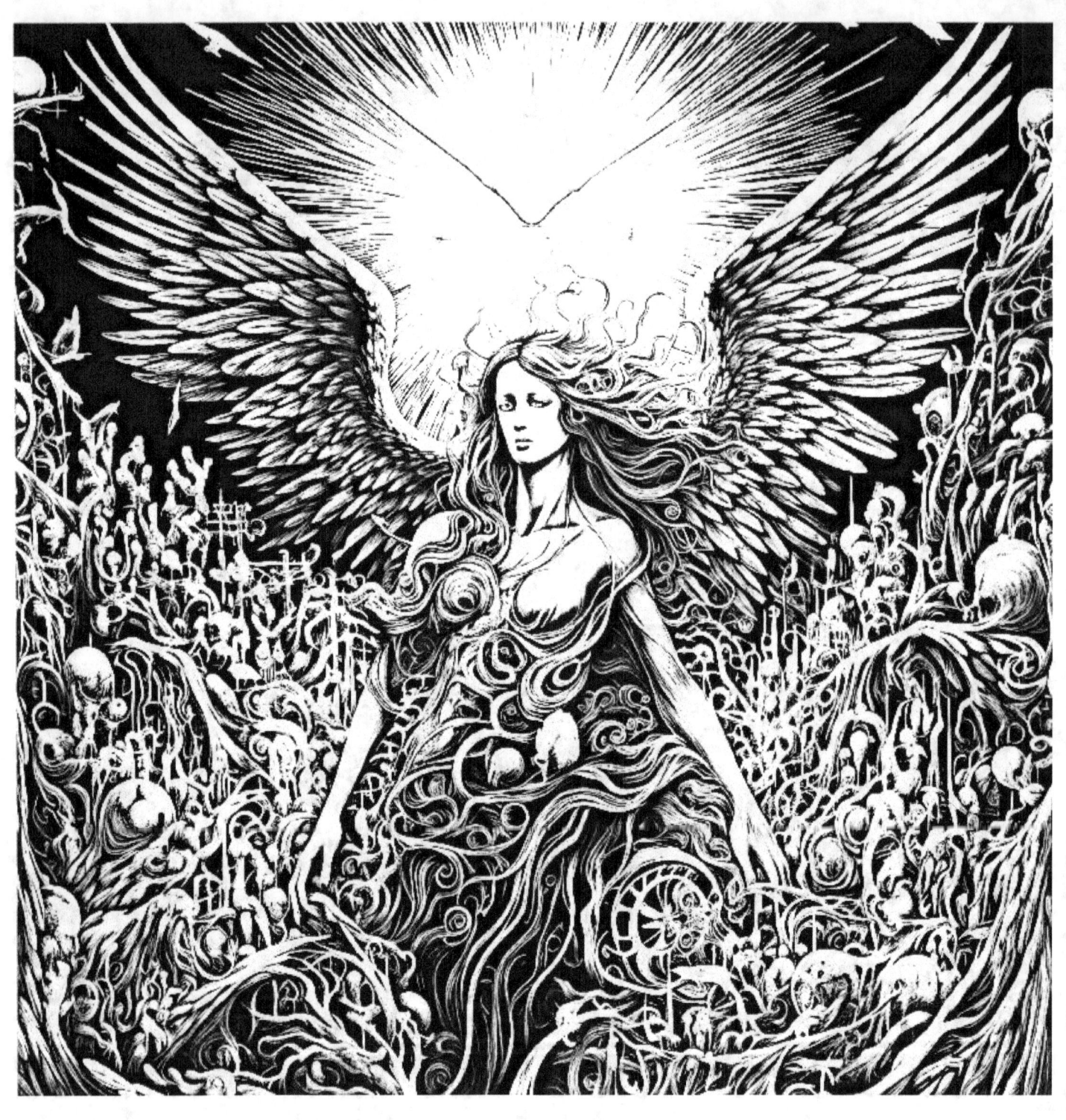

Exodus 14:19

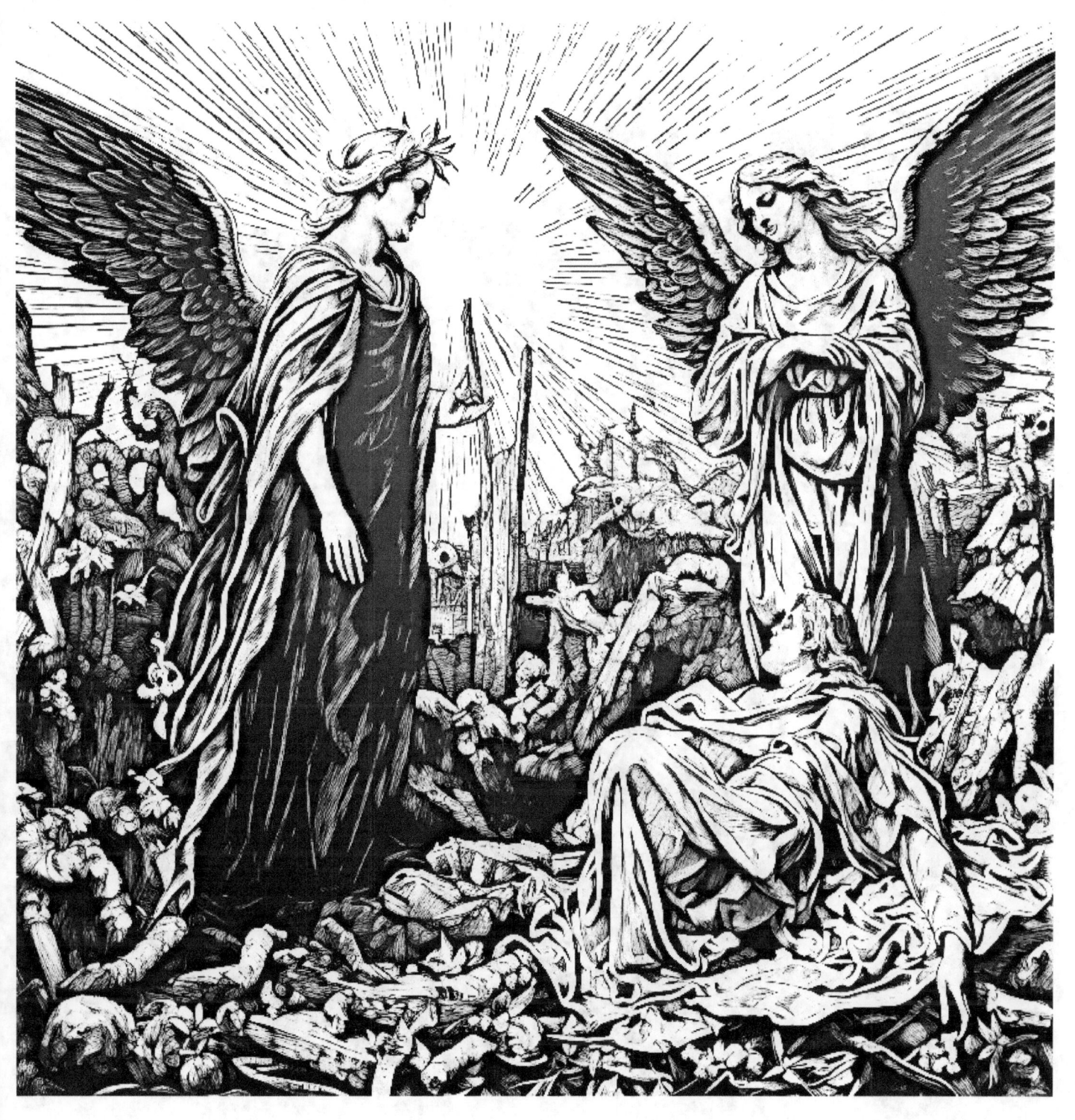

Hebrews 2:2

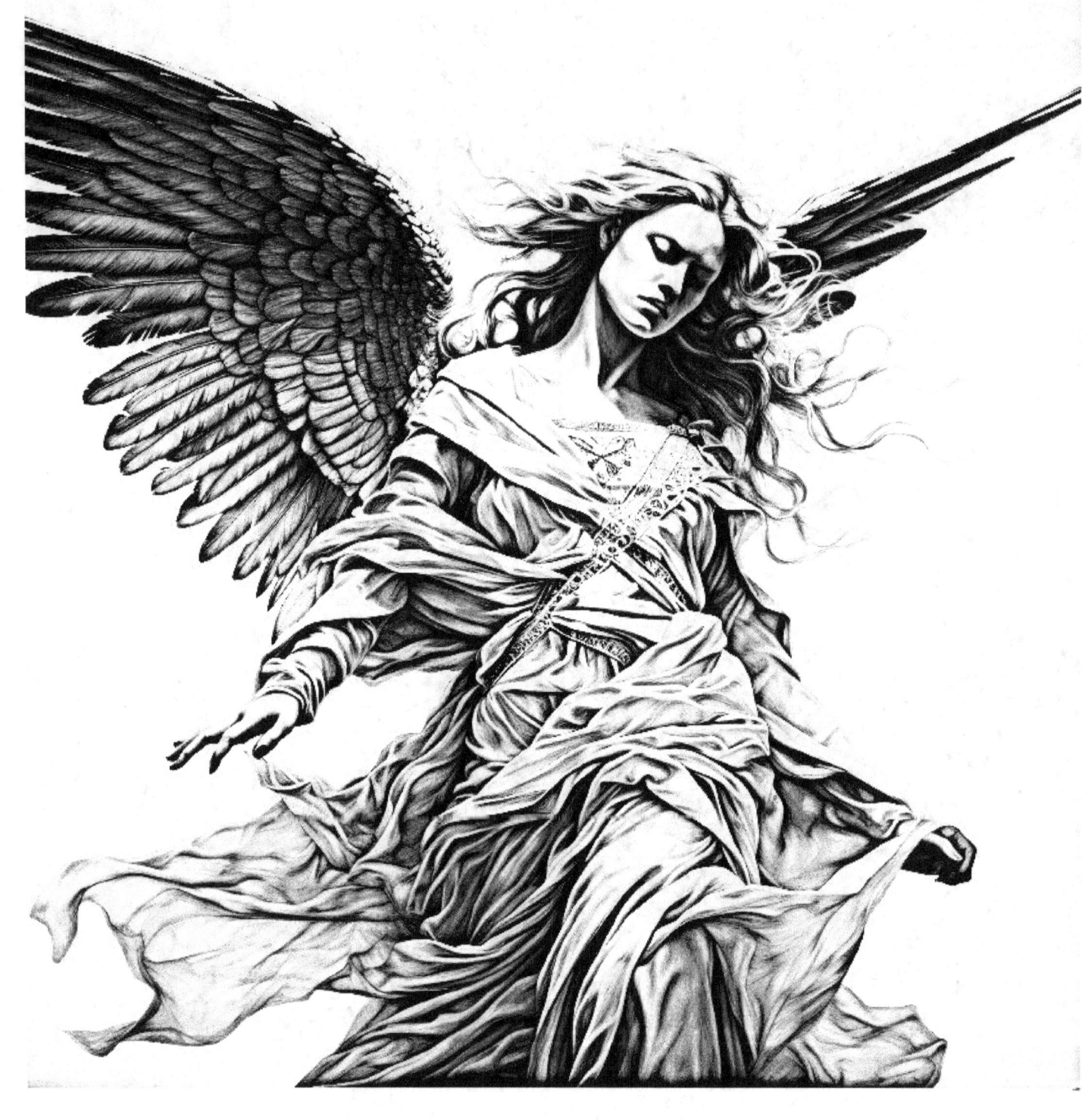

Luke 1:11-20

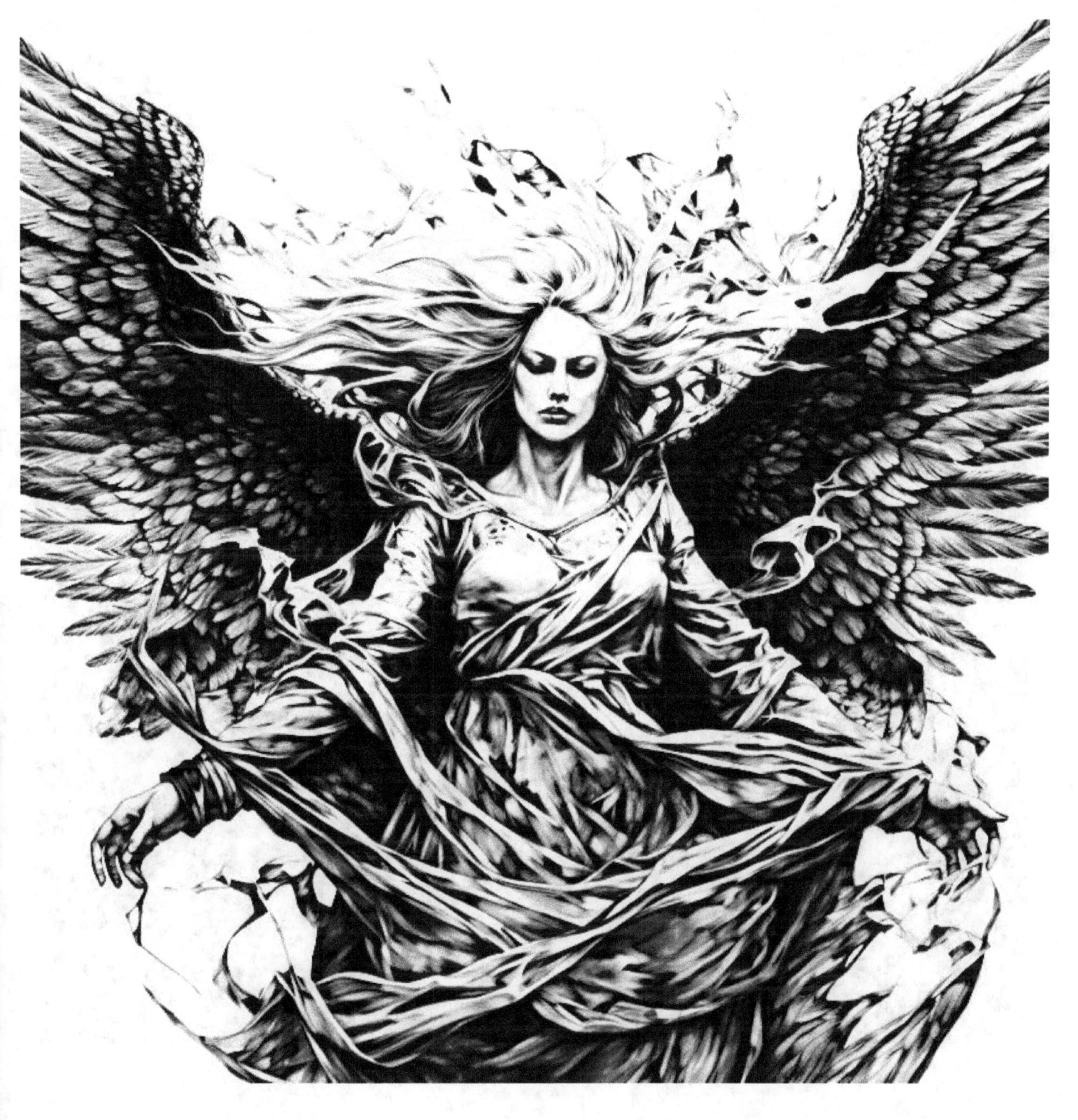

Jude 6

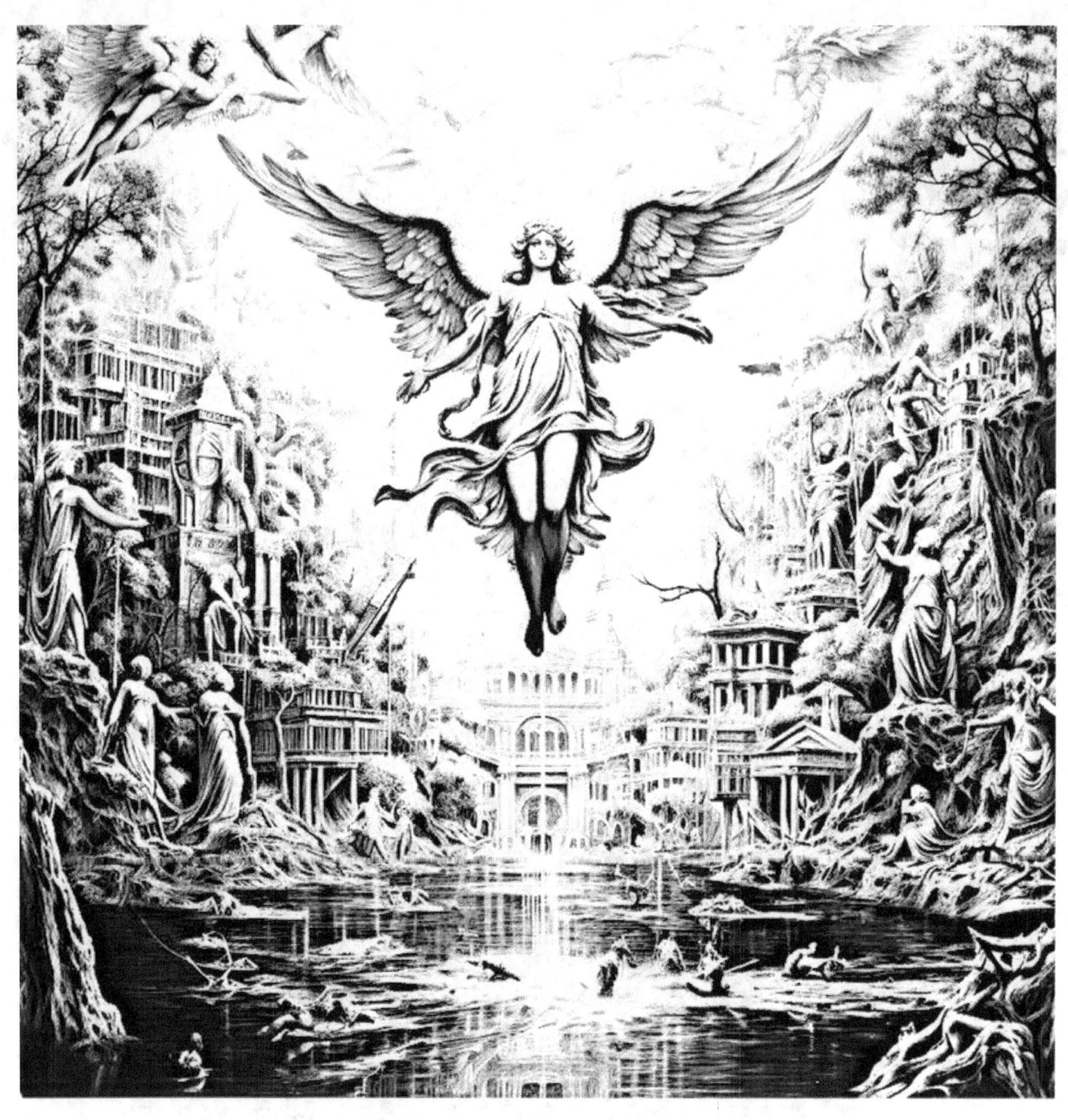

Daniel 9:21

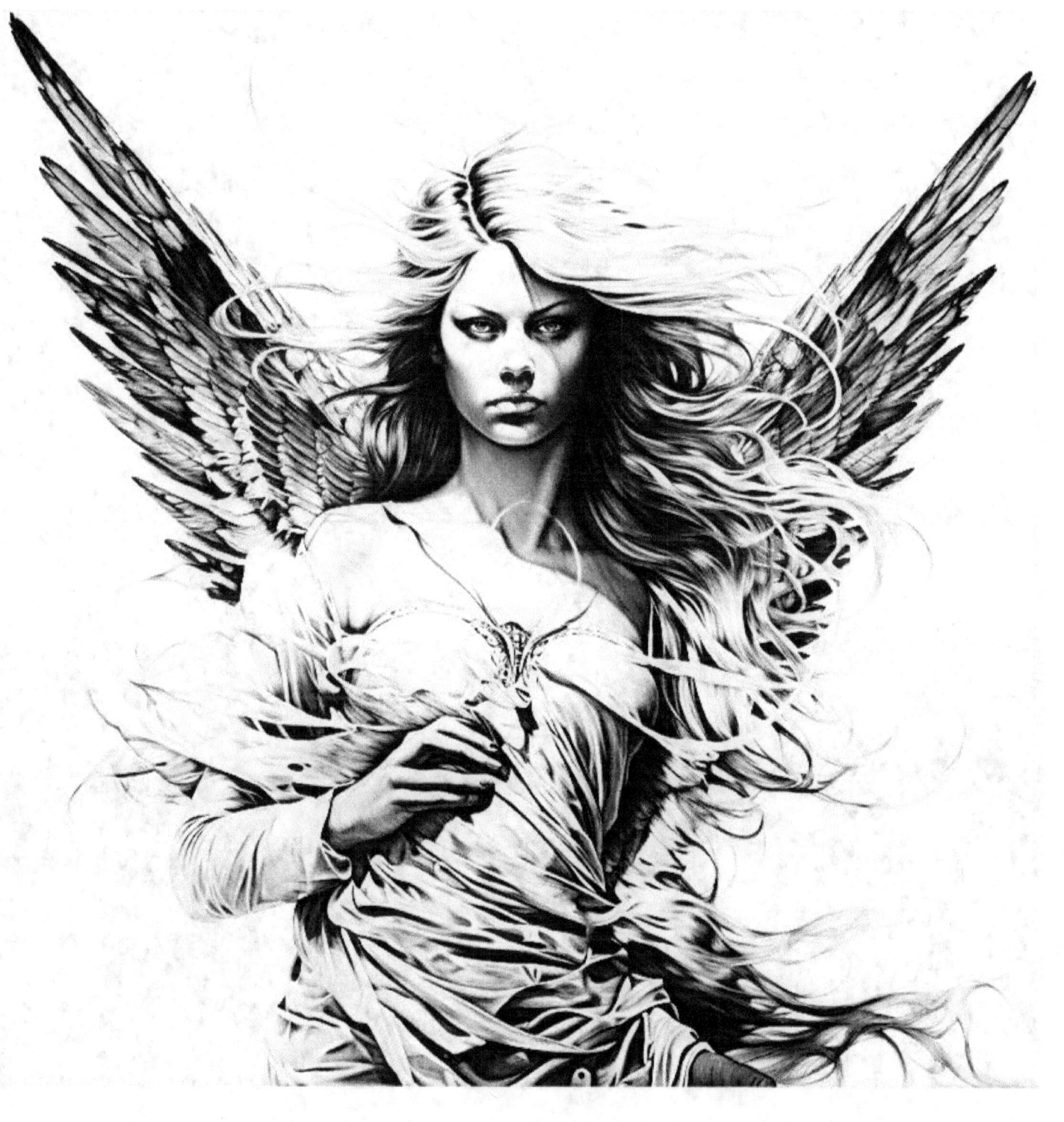

2 Samuel 14:20

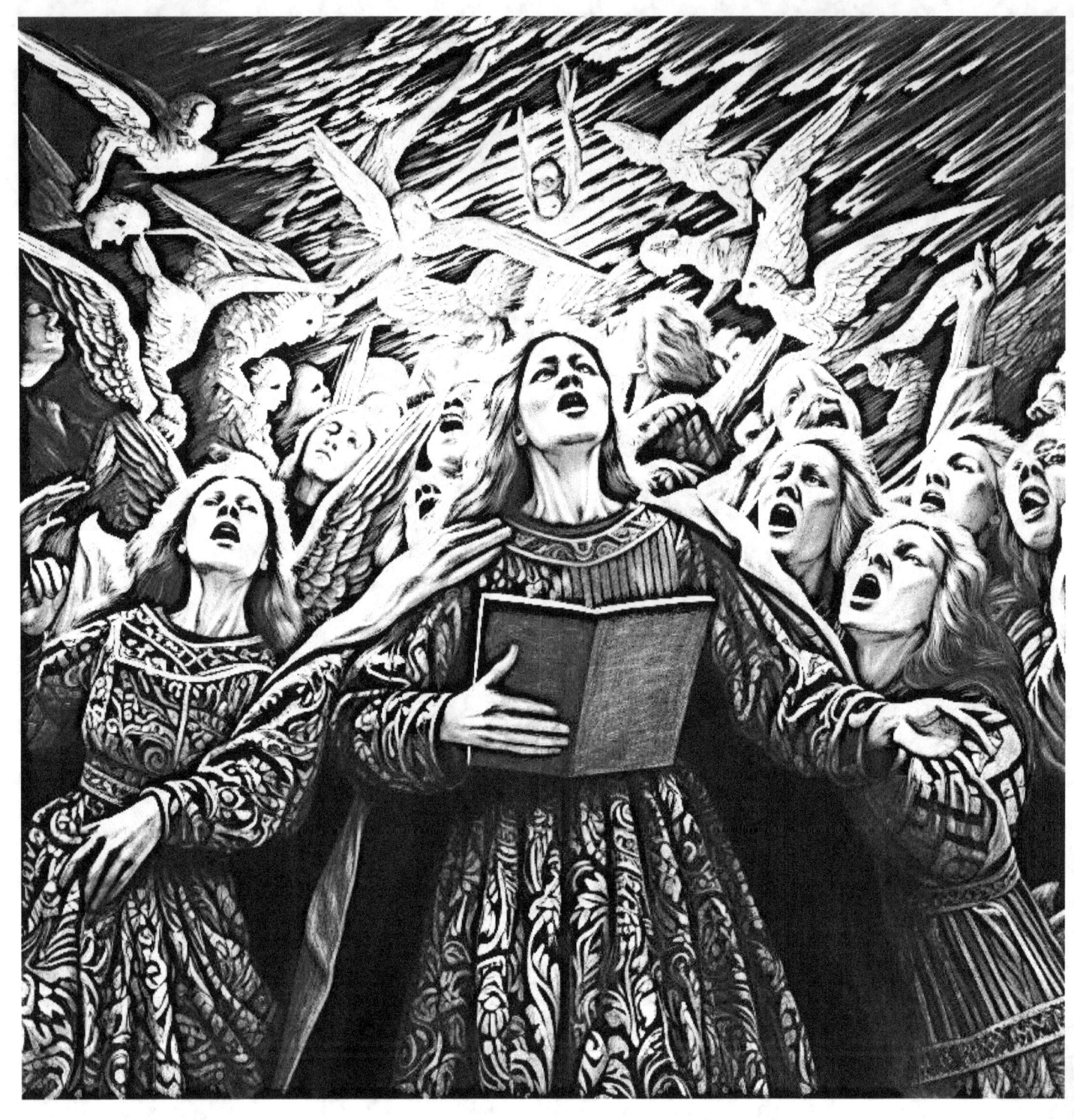

Matthew 13:41

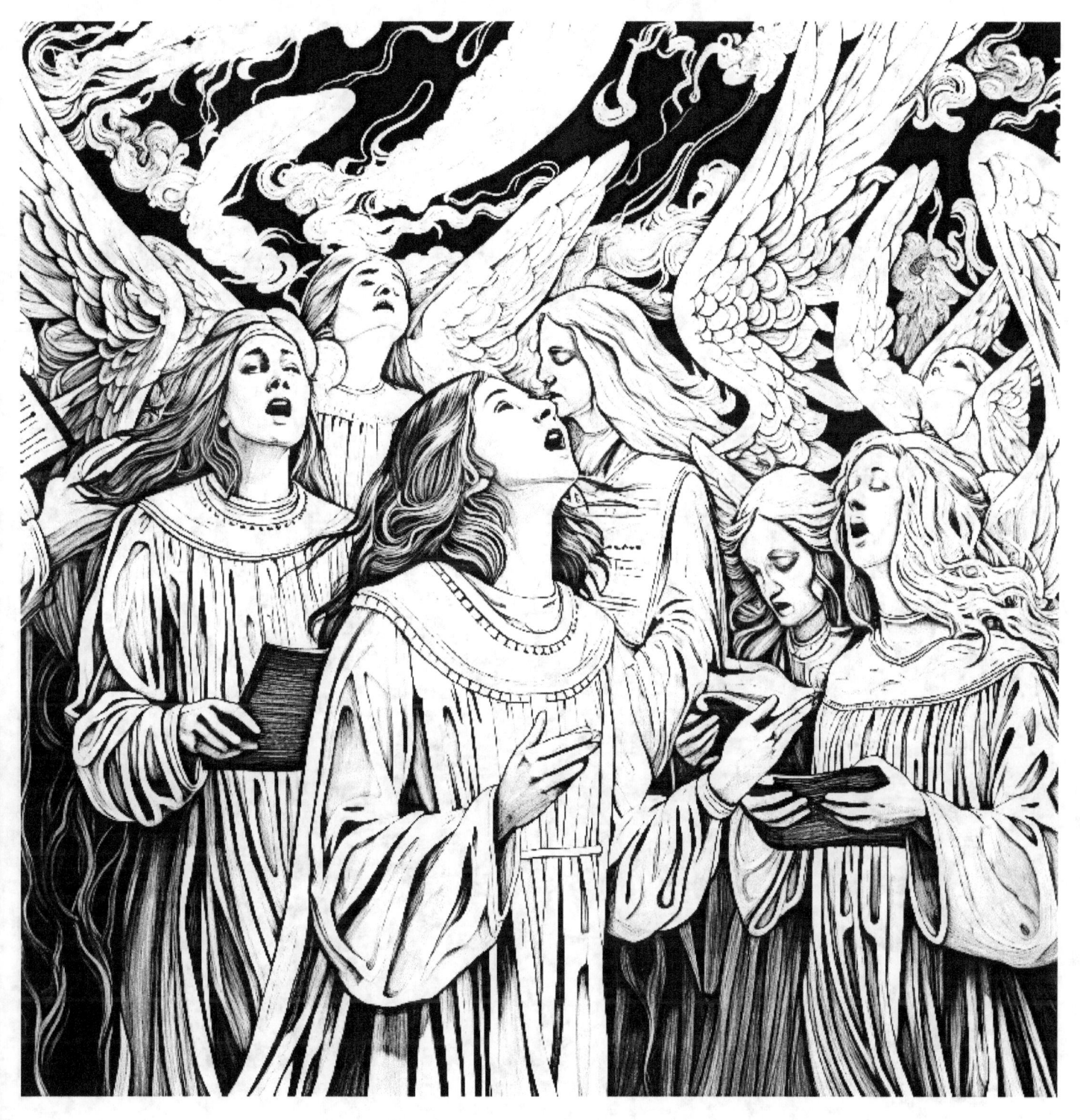

Matthew 24:31

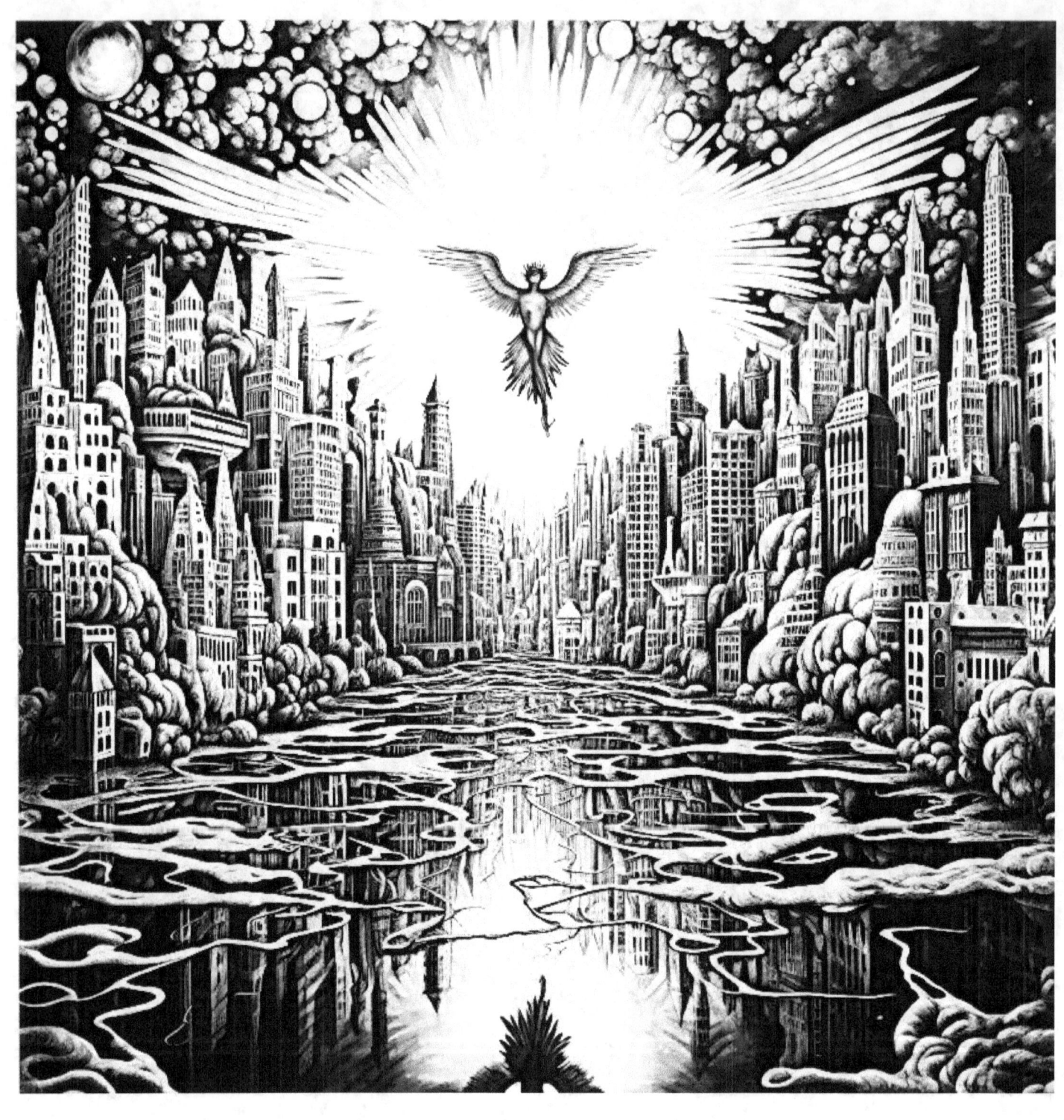

Revelation 14:6

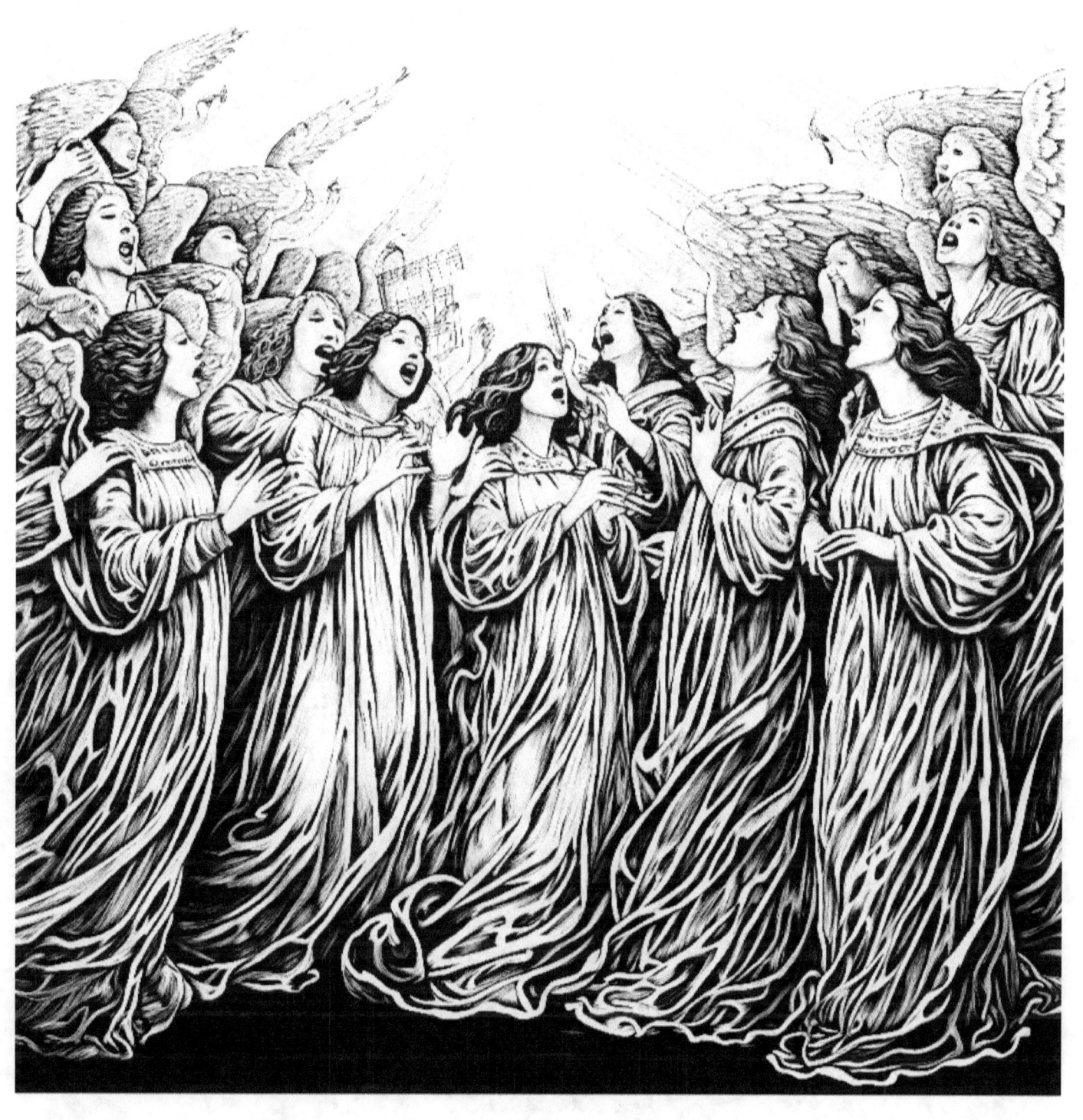

Luke 20:35-36

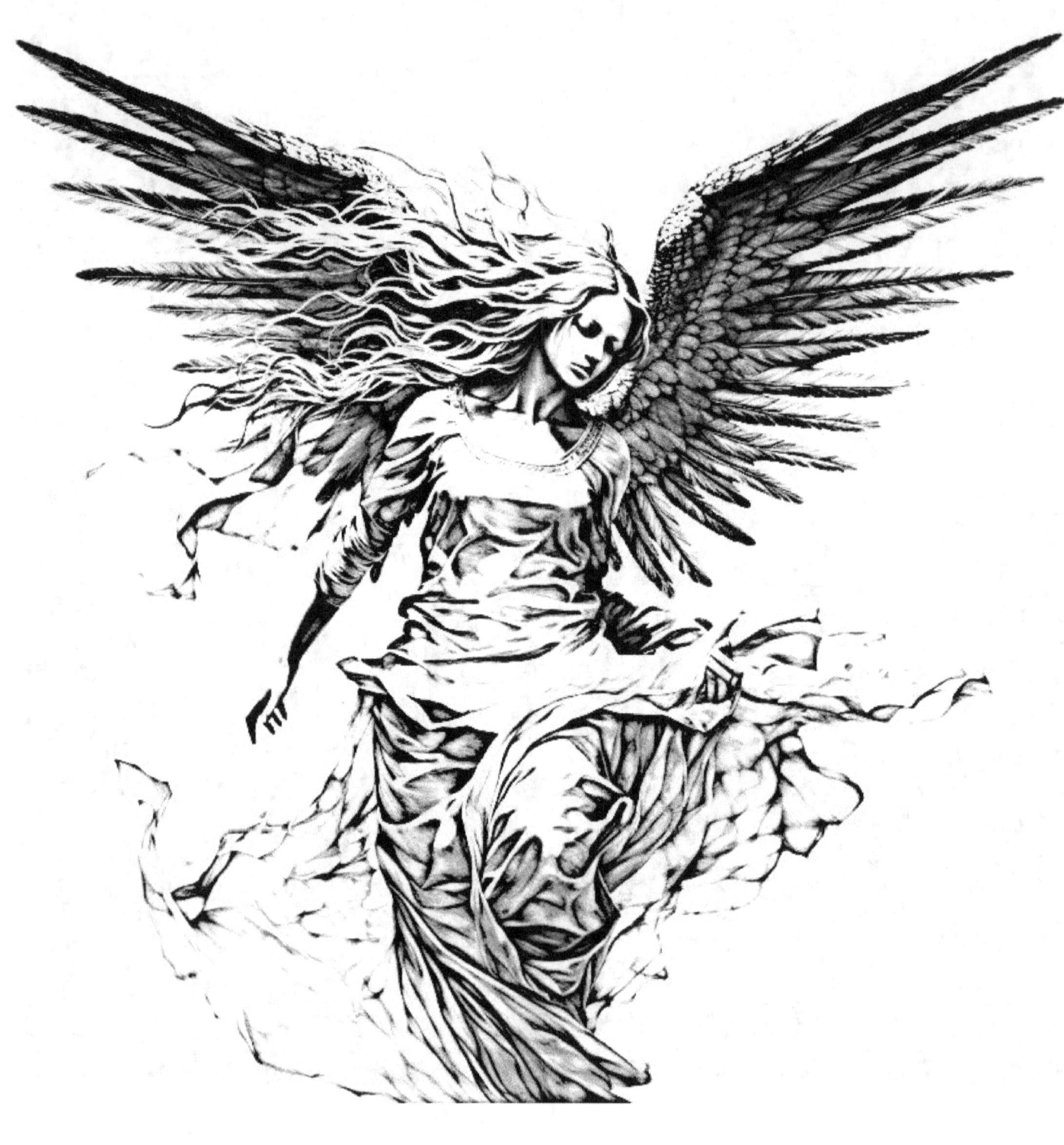

acts 12:15

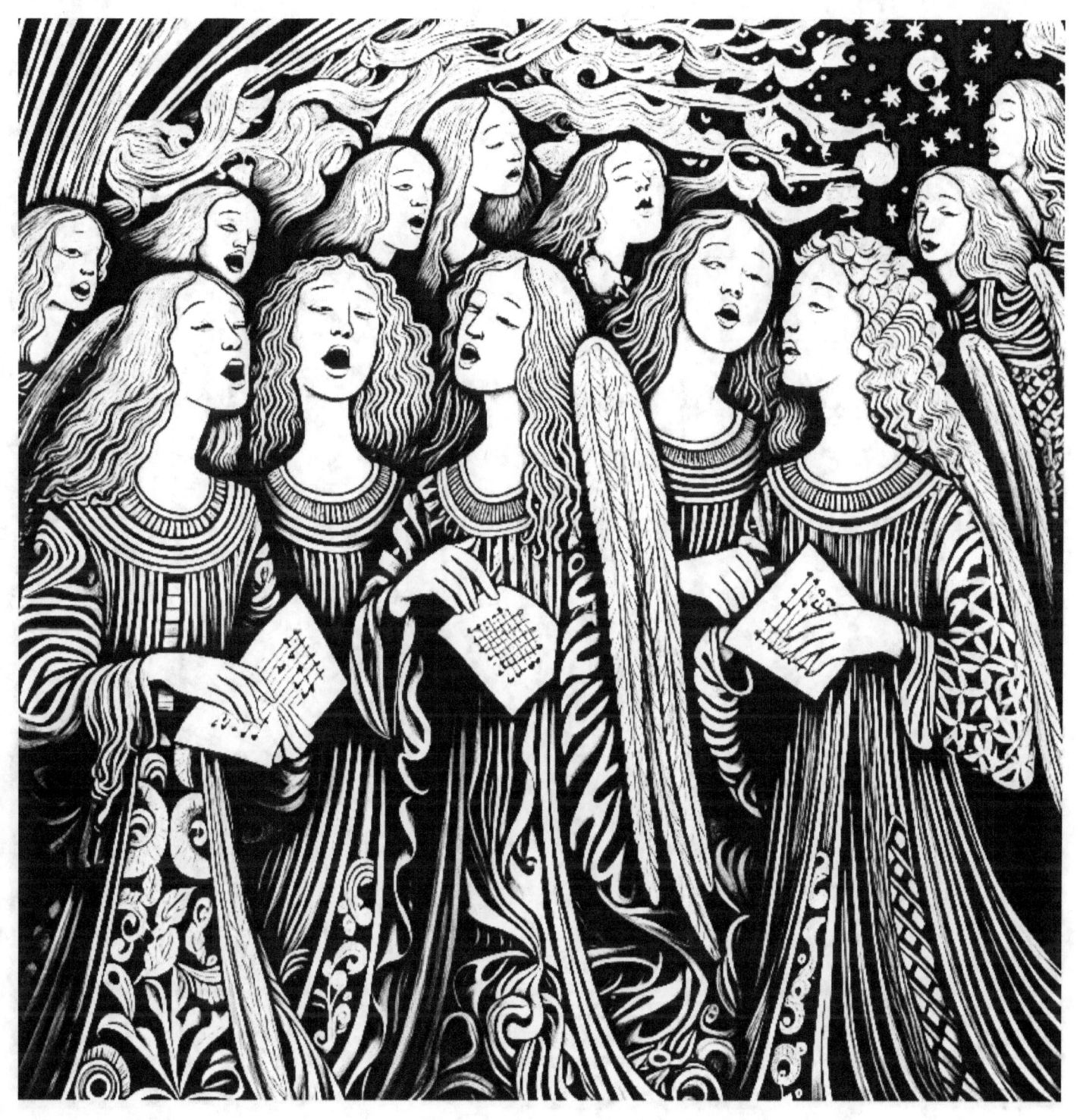

Revelation 5:11-12

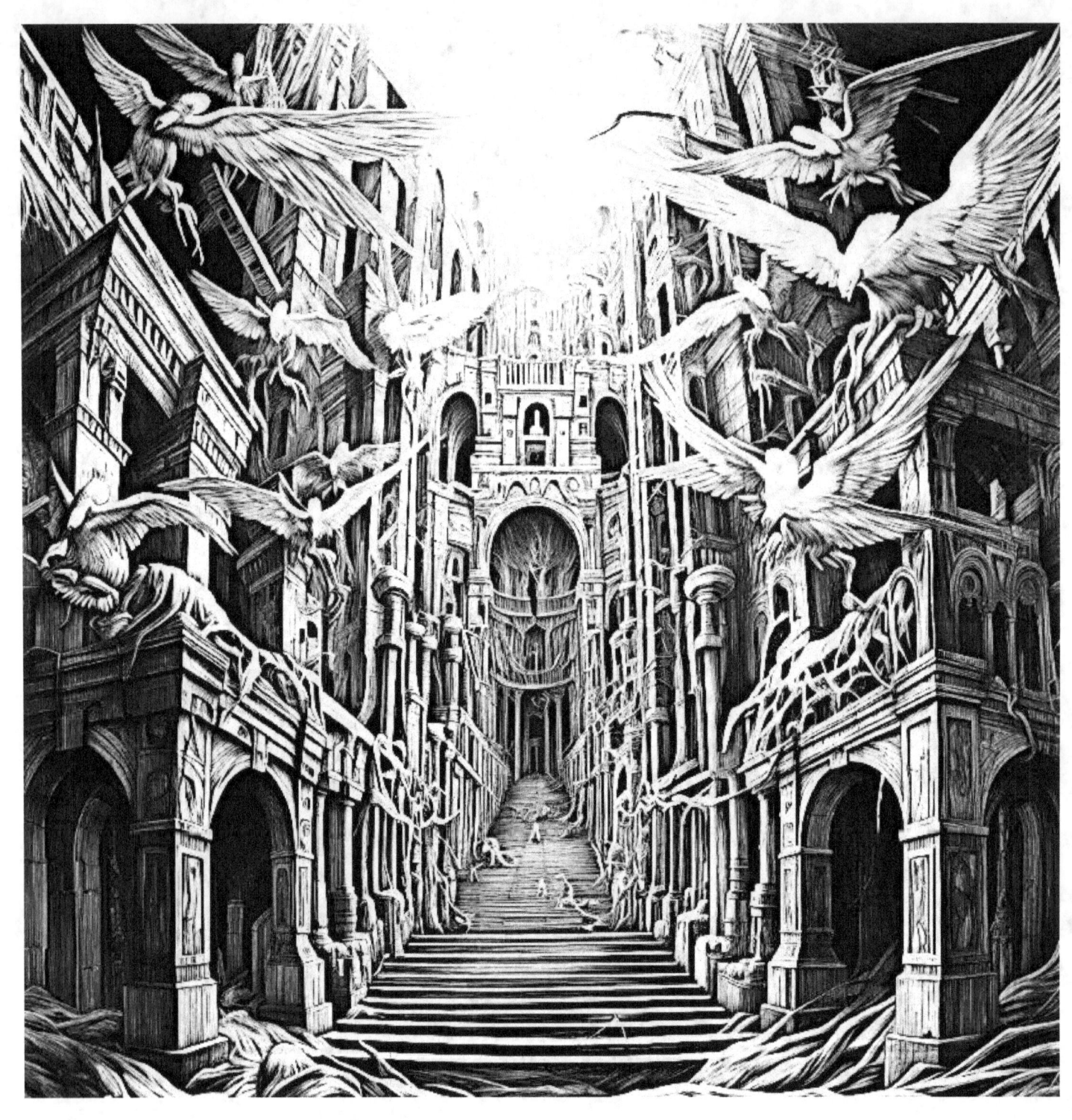

Romans 8:38-39

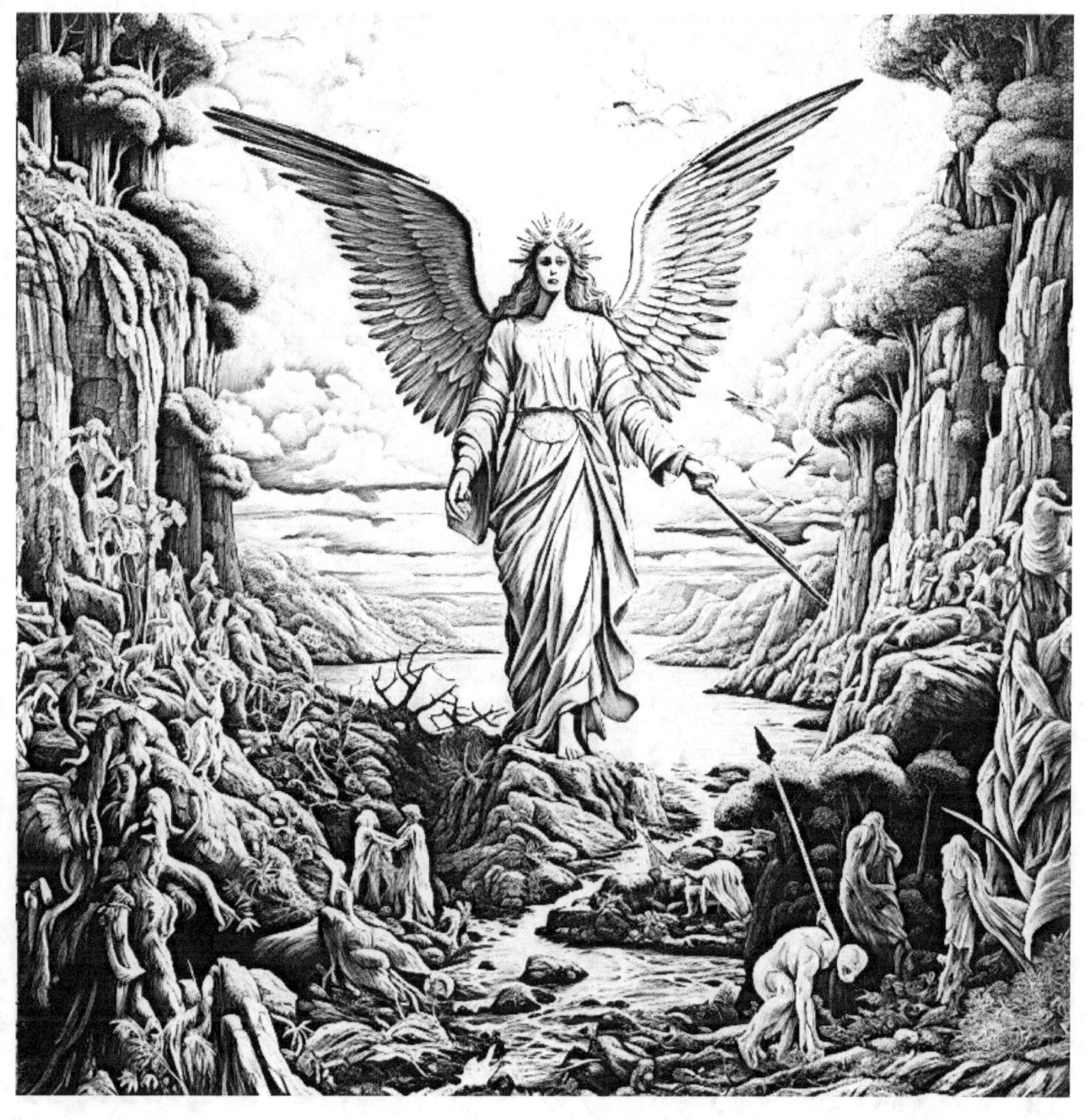

Luke 2:10

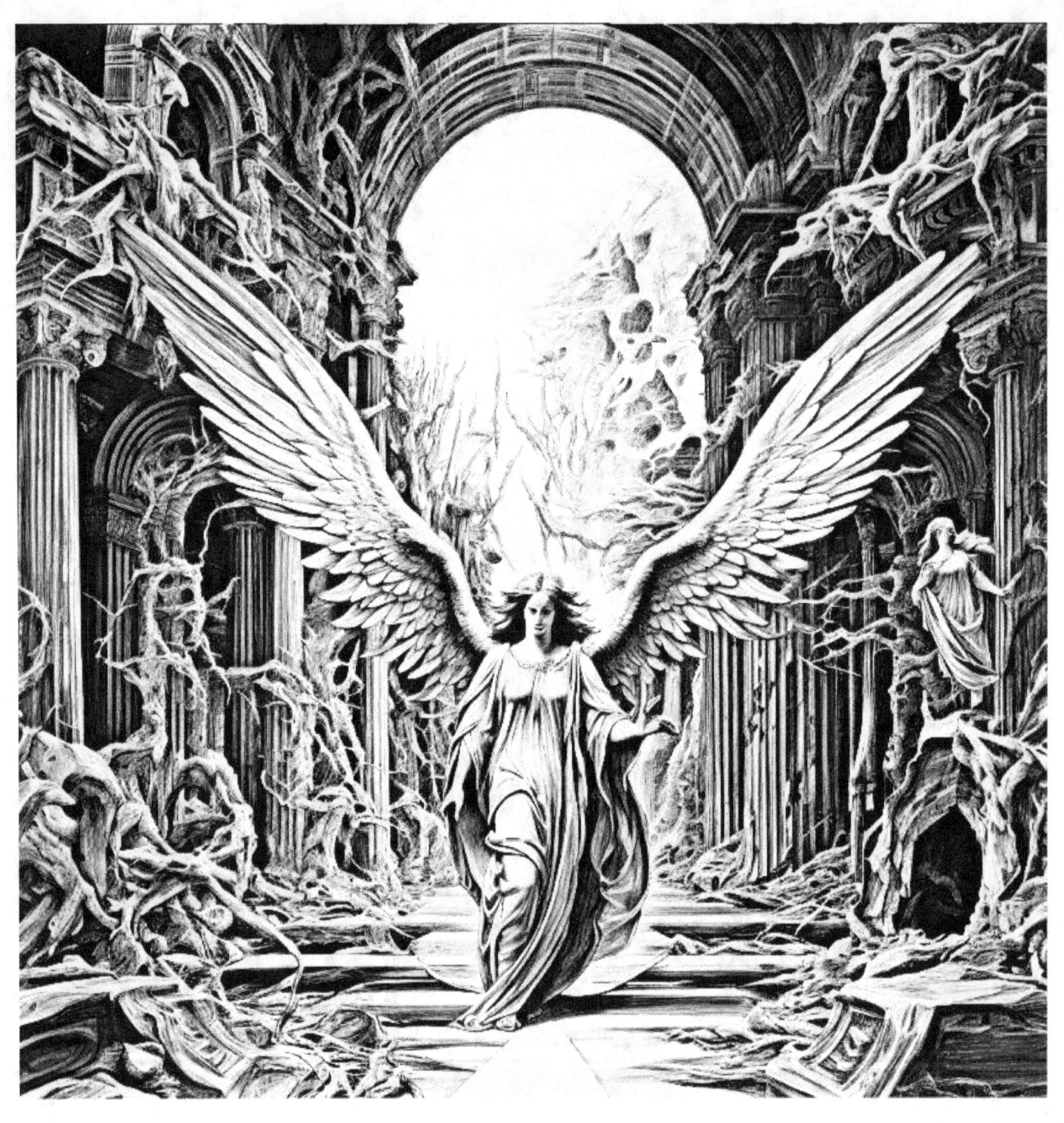

Psalm 34:7

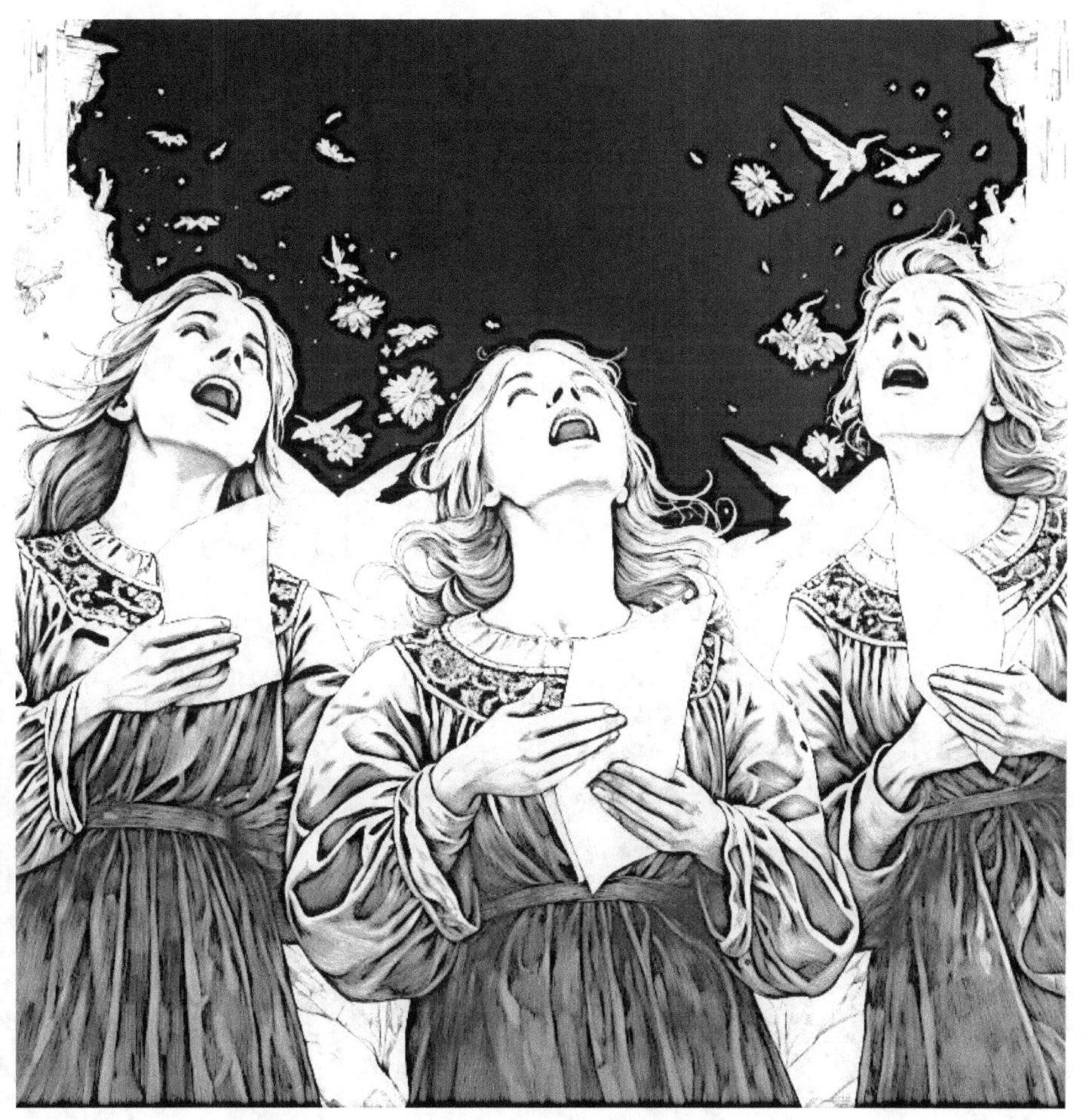

Psalm 148:2

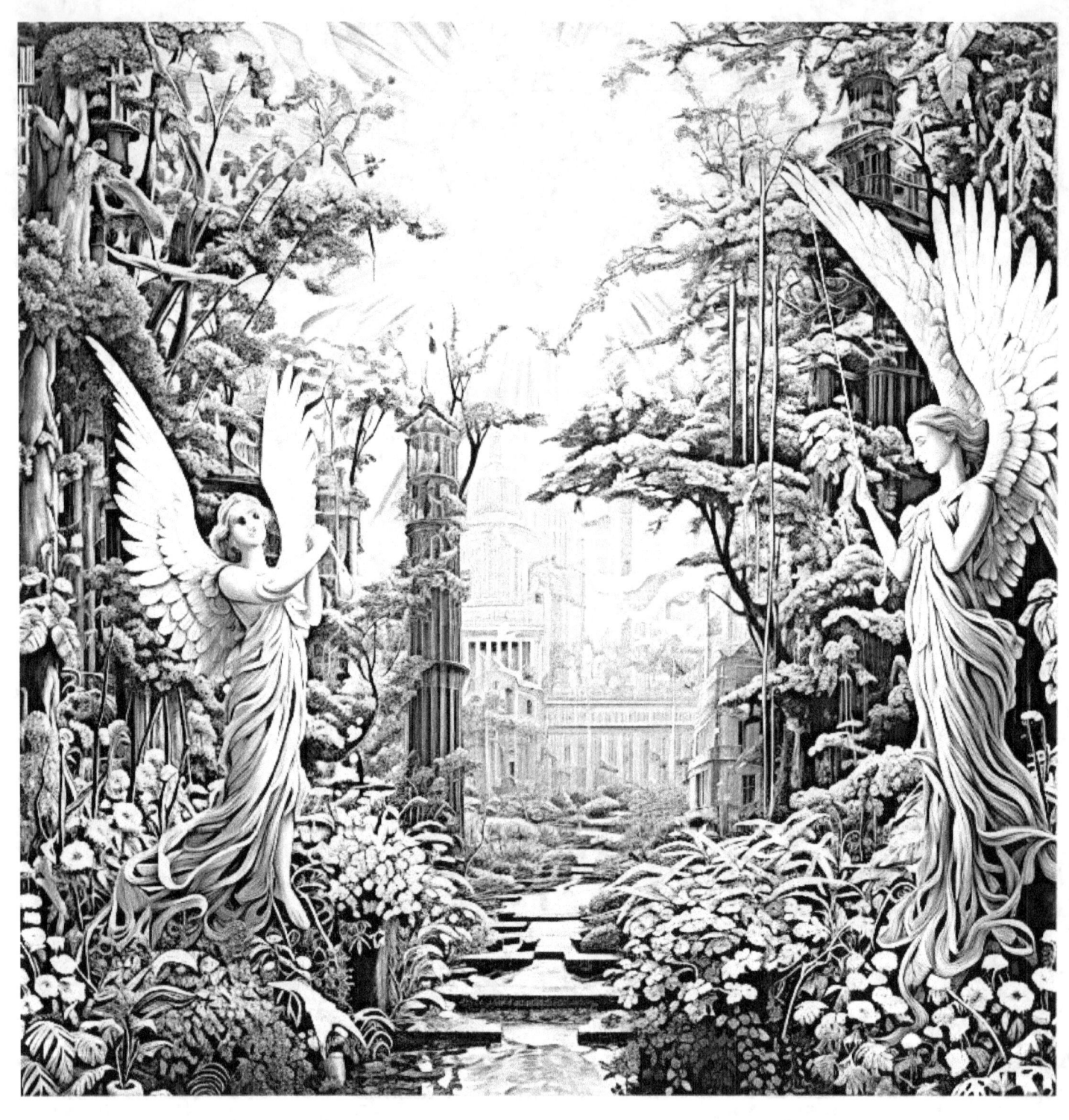

1 Corinthians 13:1

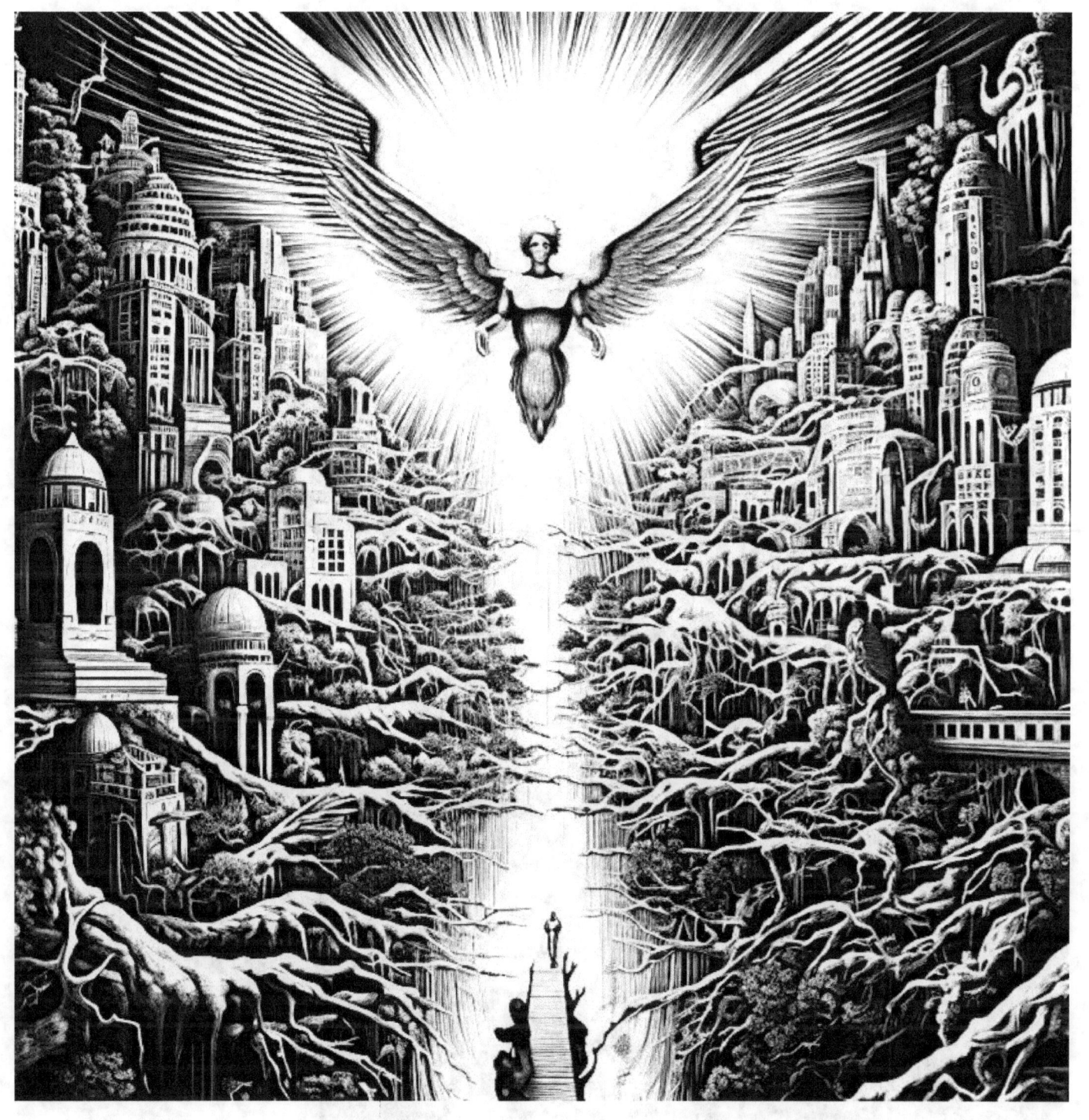

Revelation 14:6-8

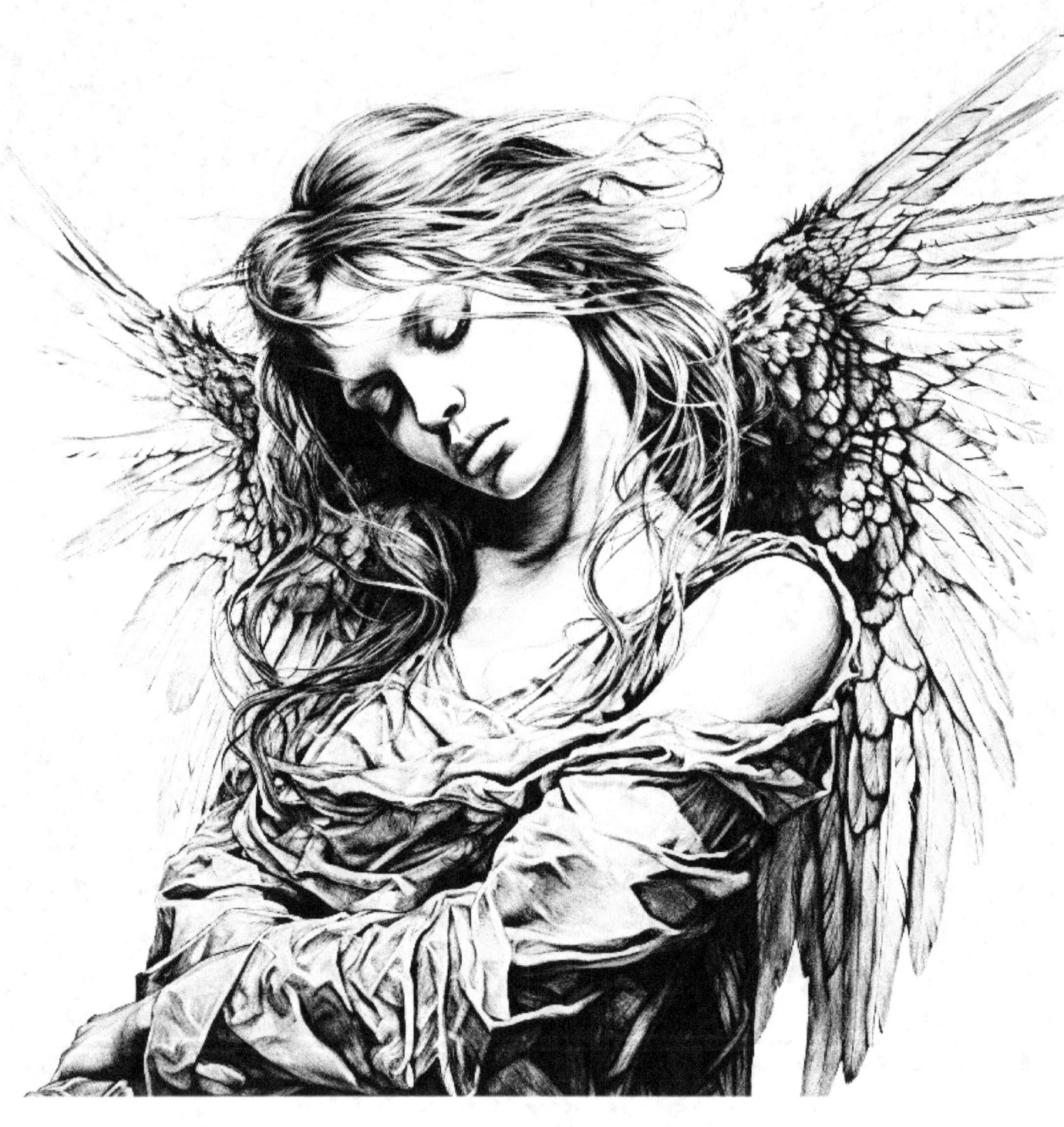

2 Samuel 14:17

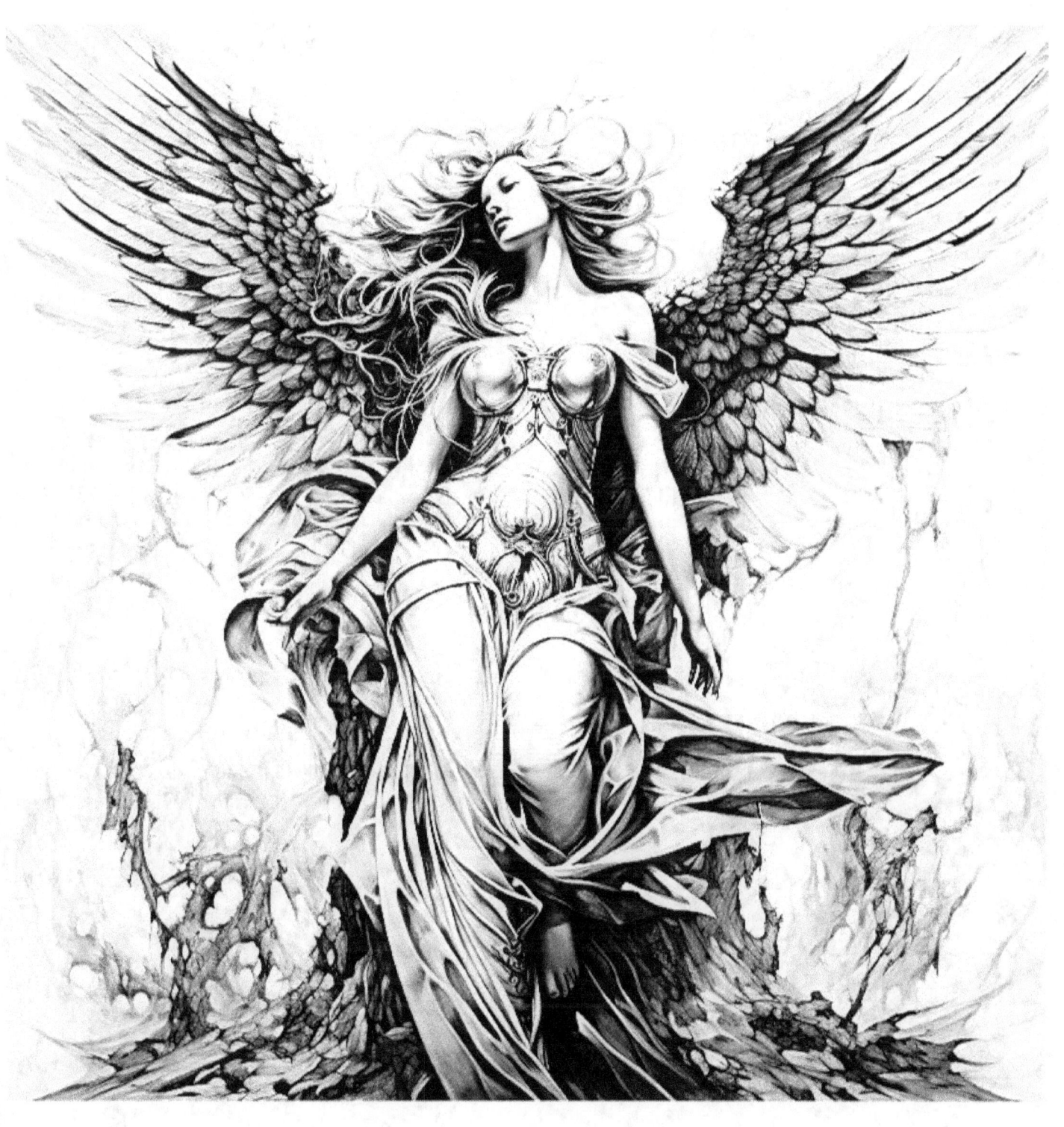

John 1:51

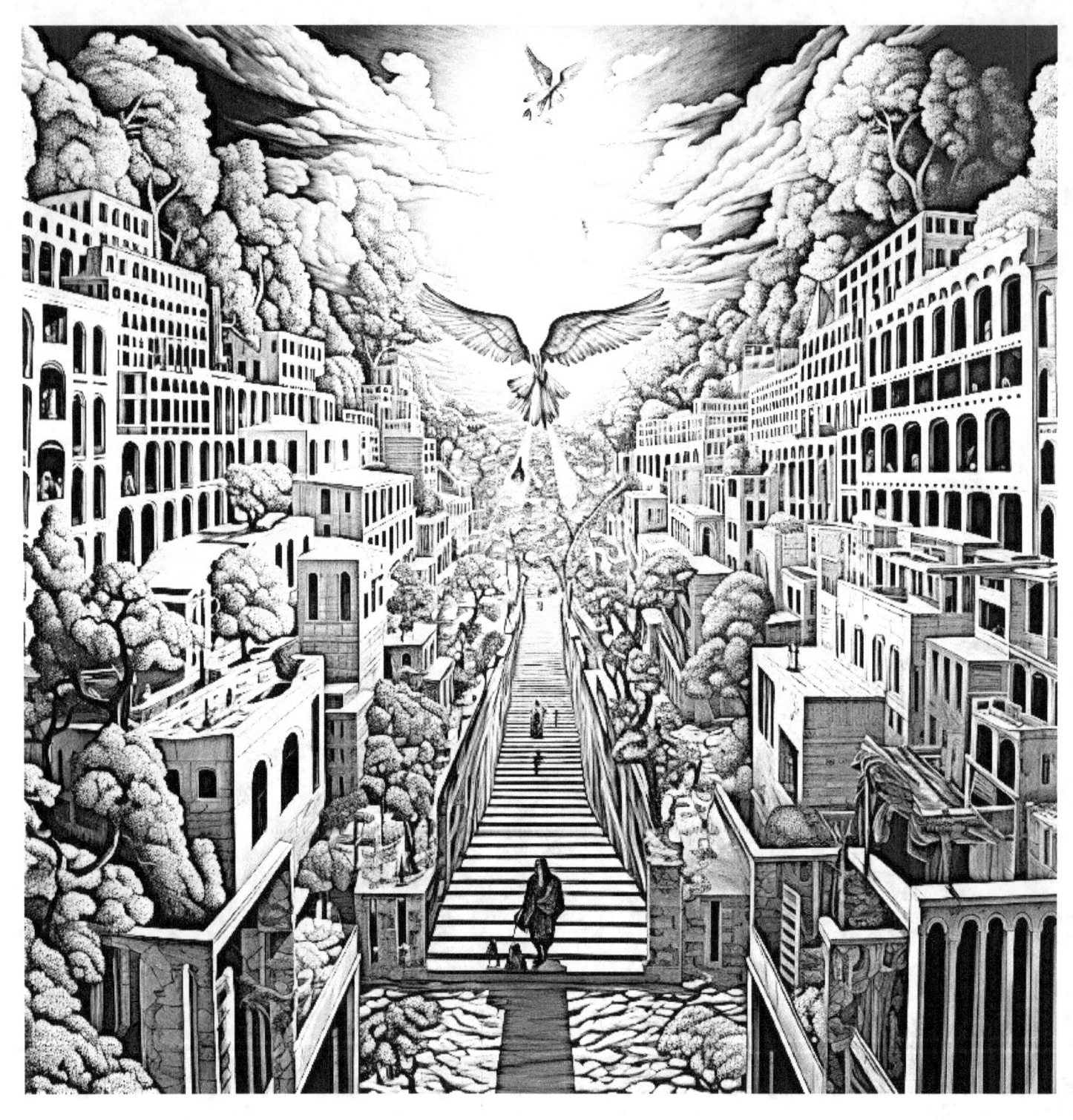

Isaiah 6:2

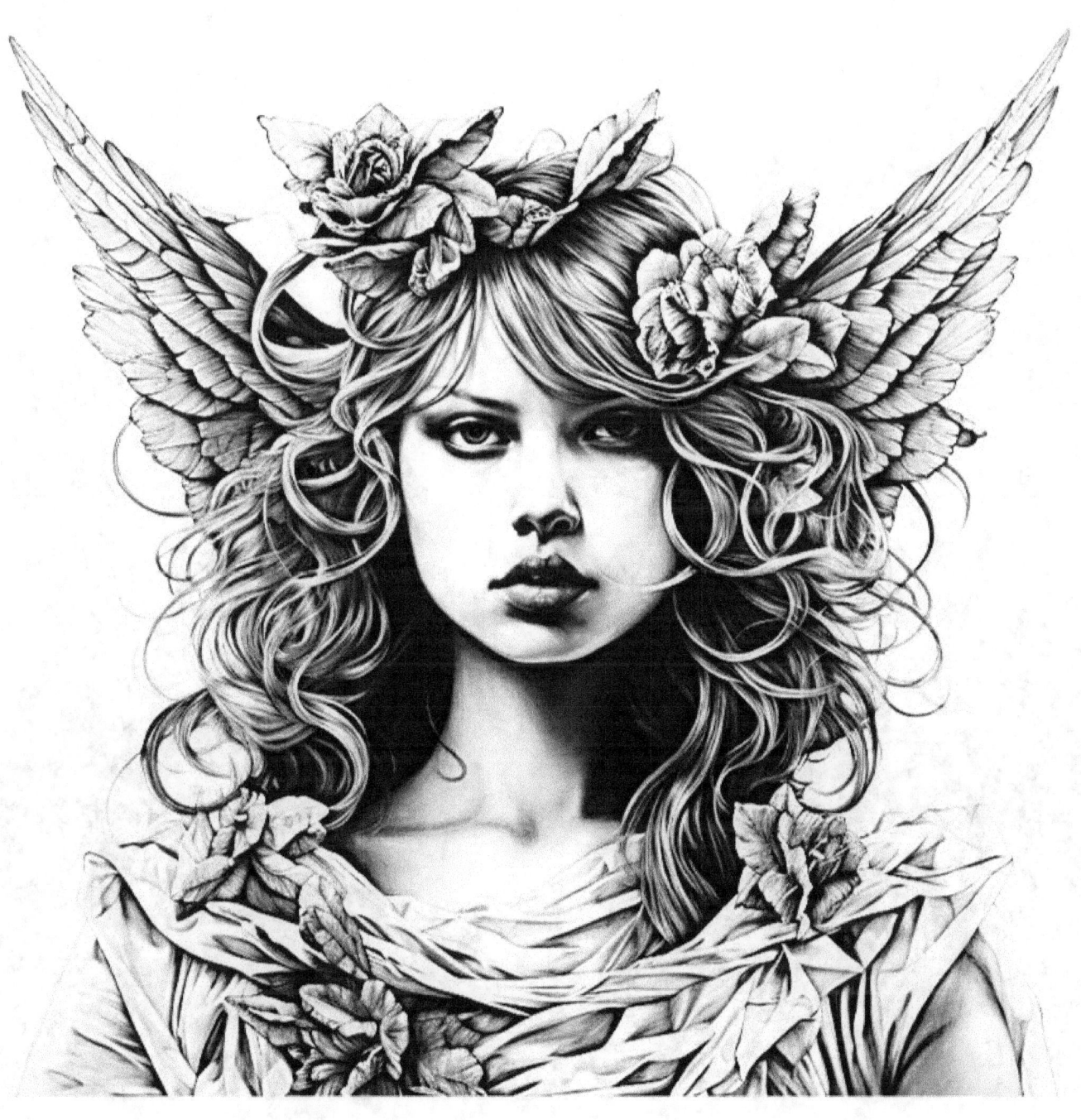

genesis 16:7

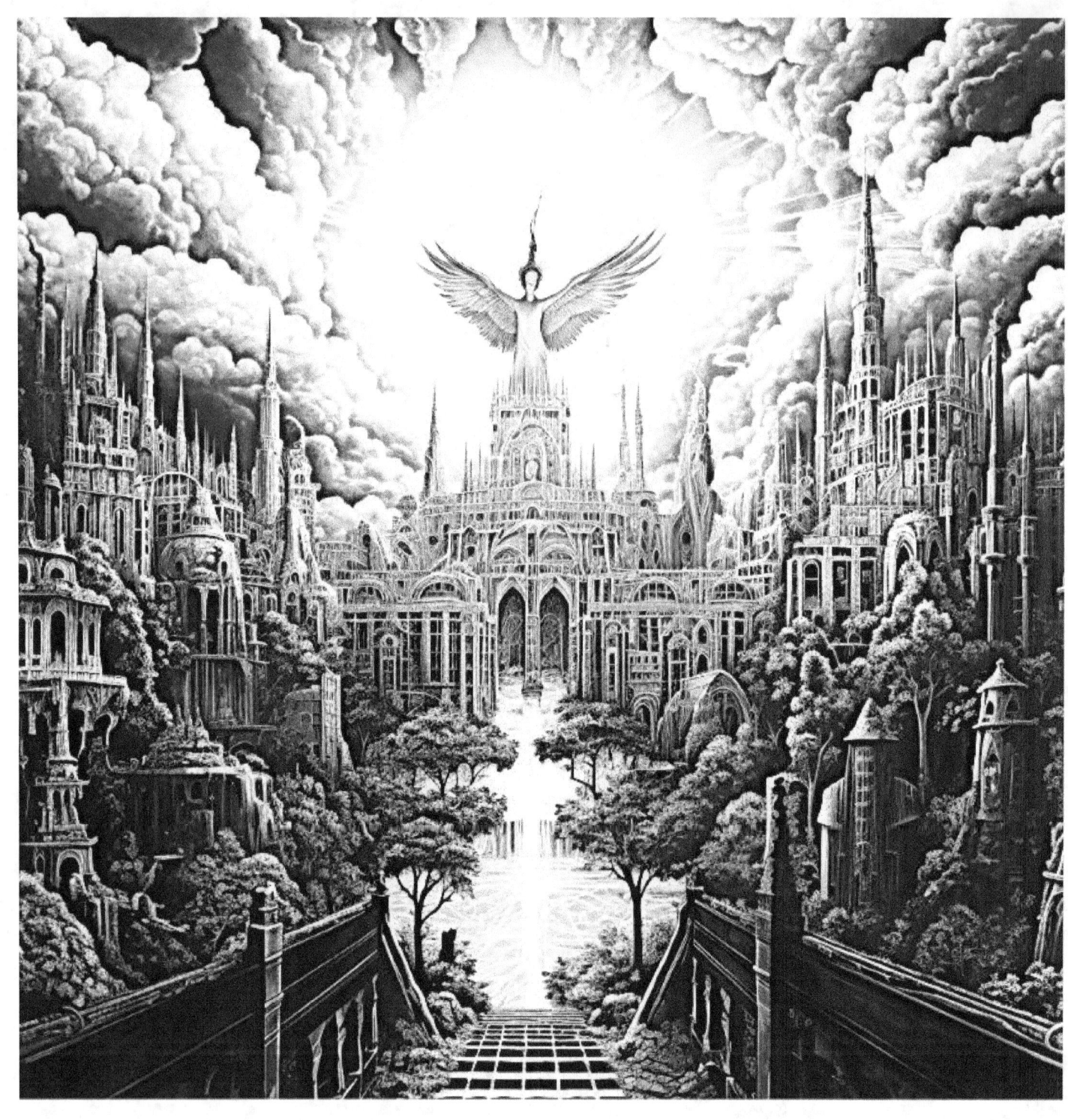

Luke 1:26

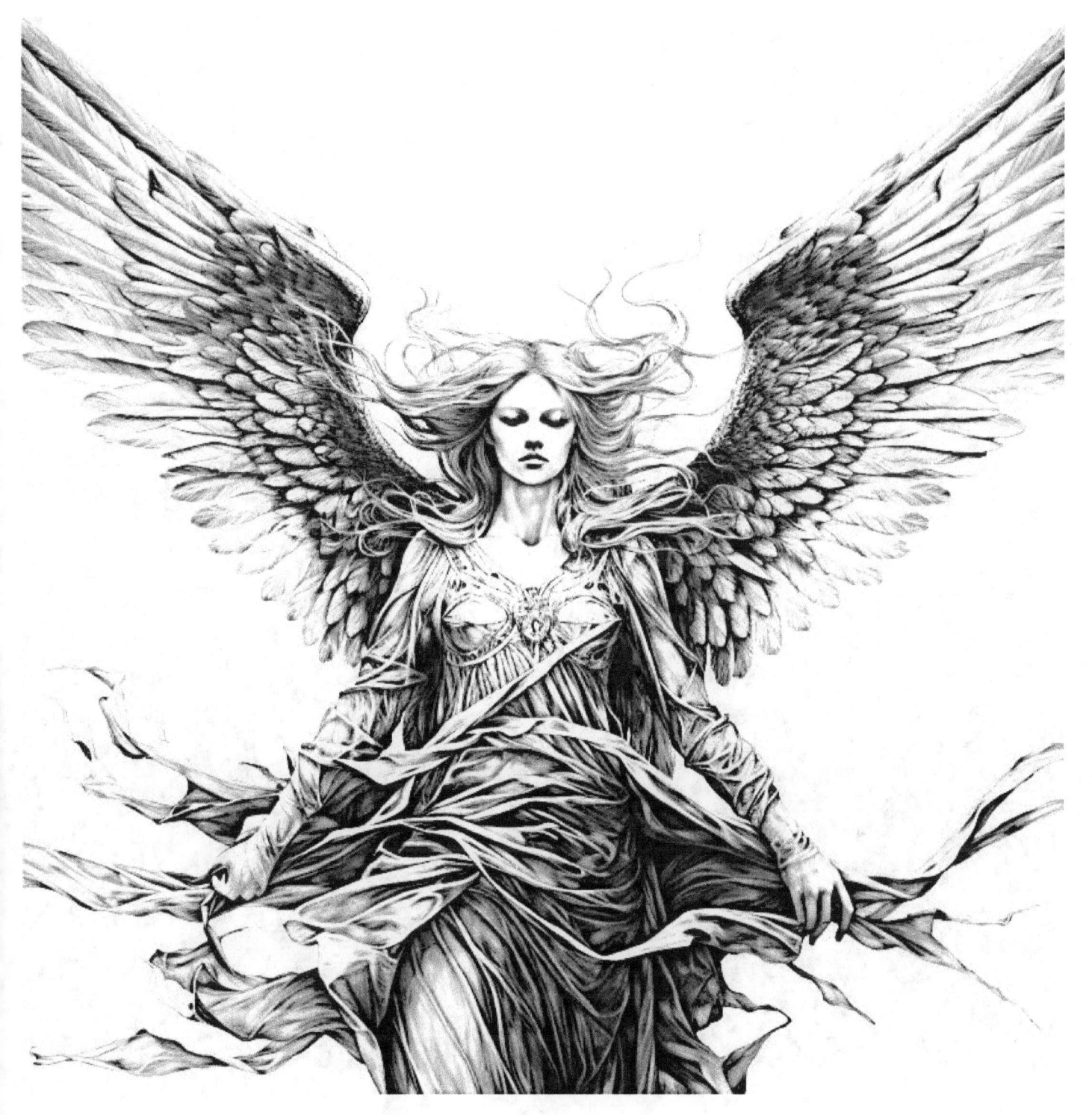

Revelation 10:1-6

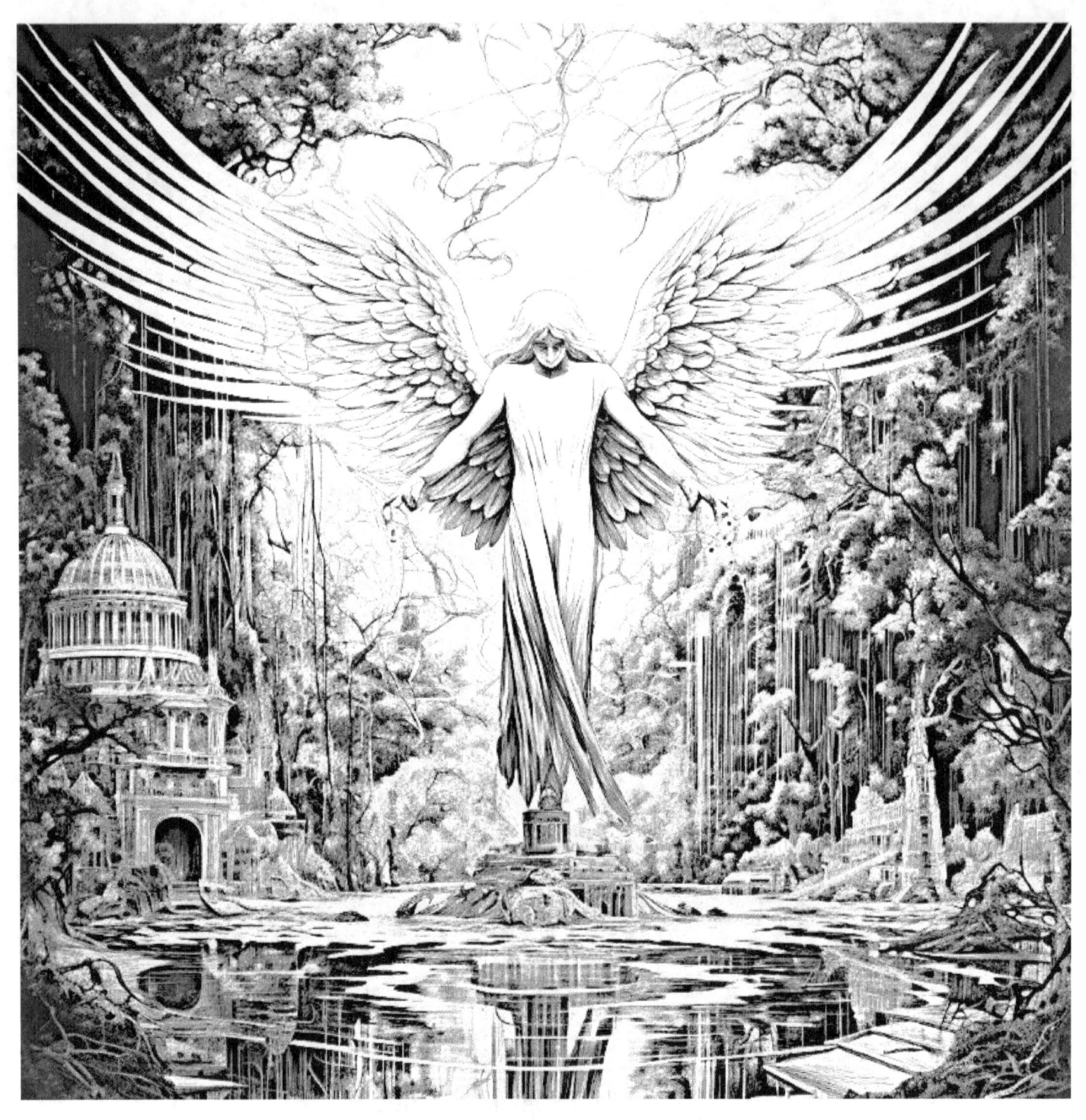

Luke 1:19-20

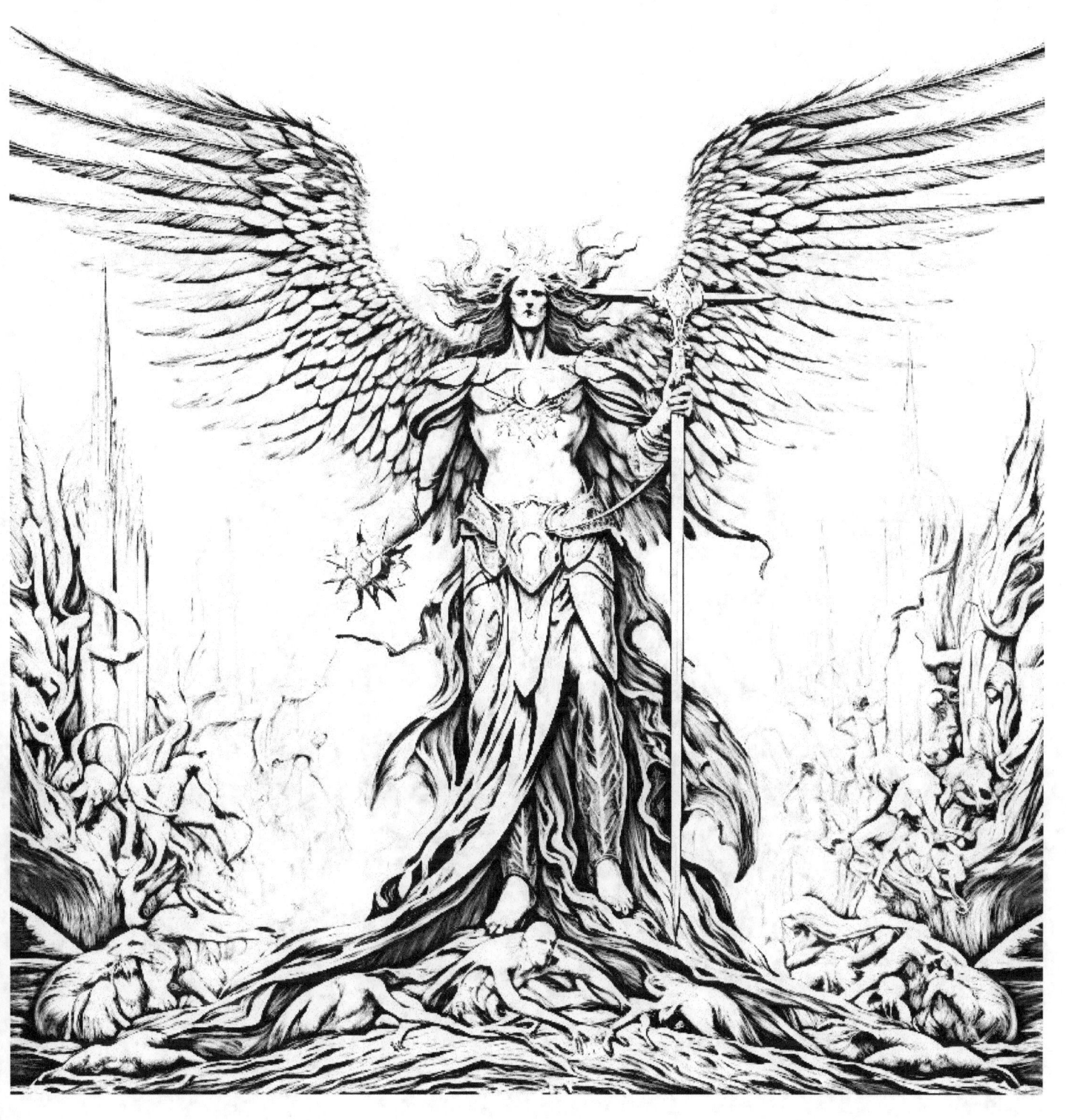

genesis 3:24

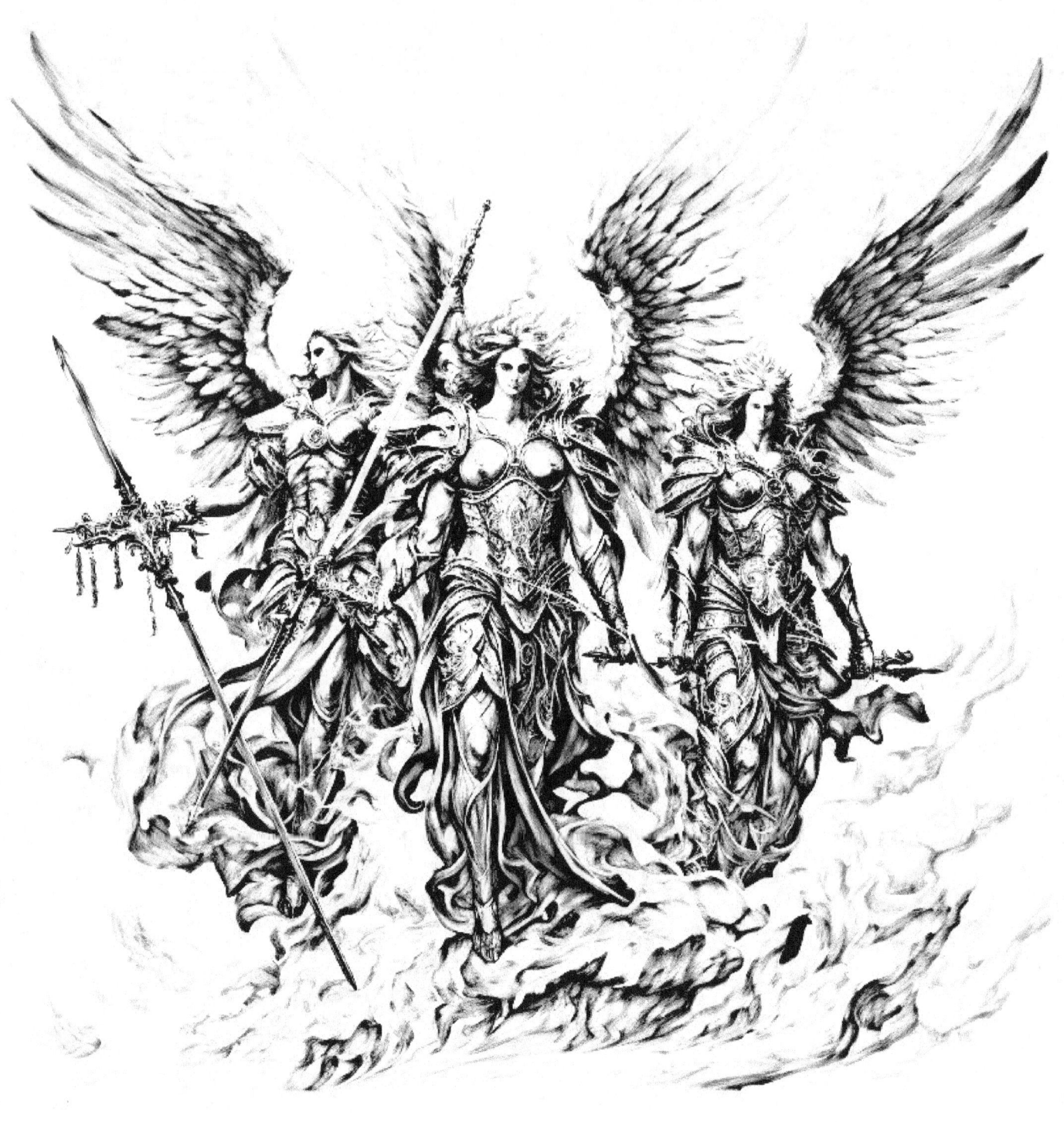

Psalm 78:49

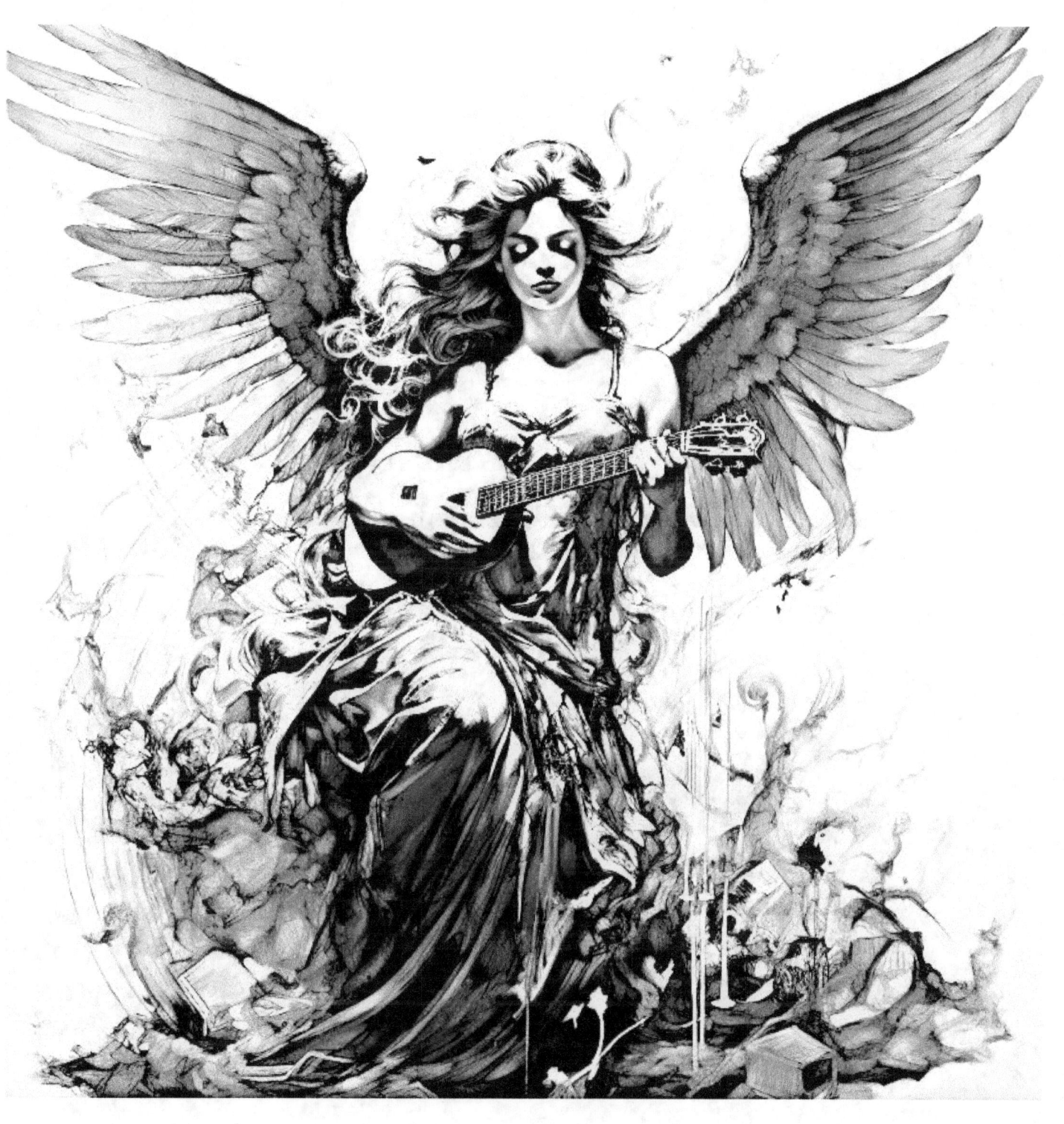

Mark 1:13

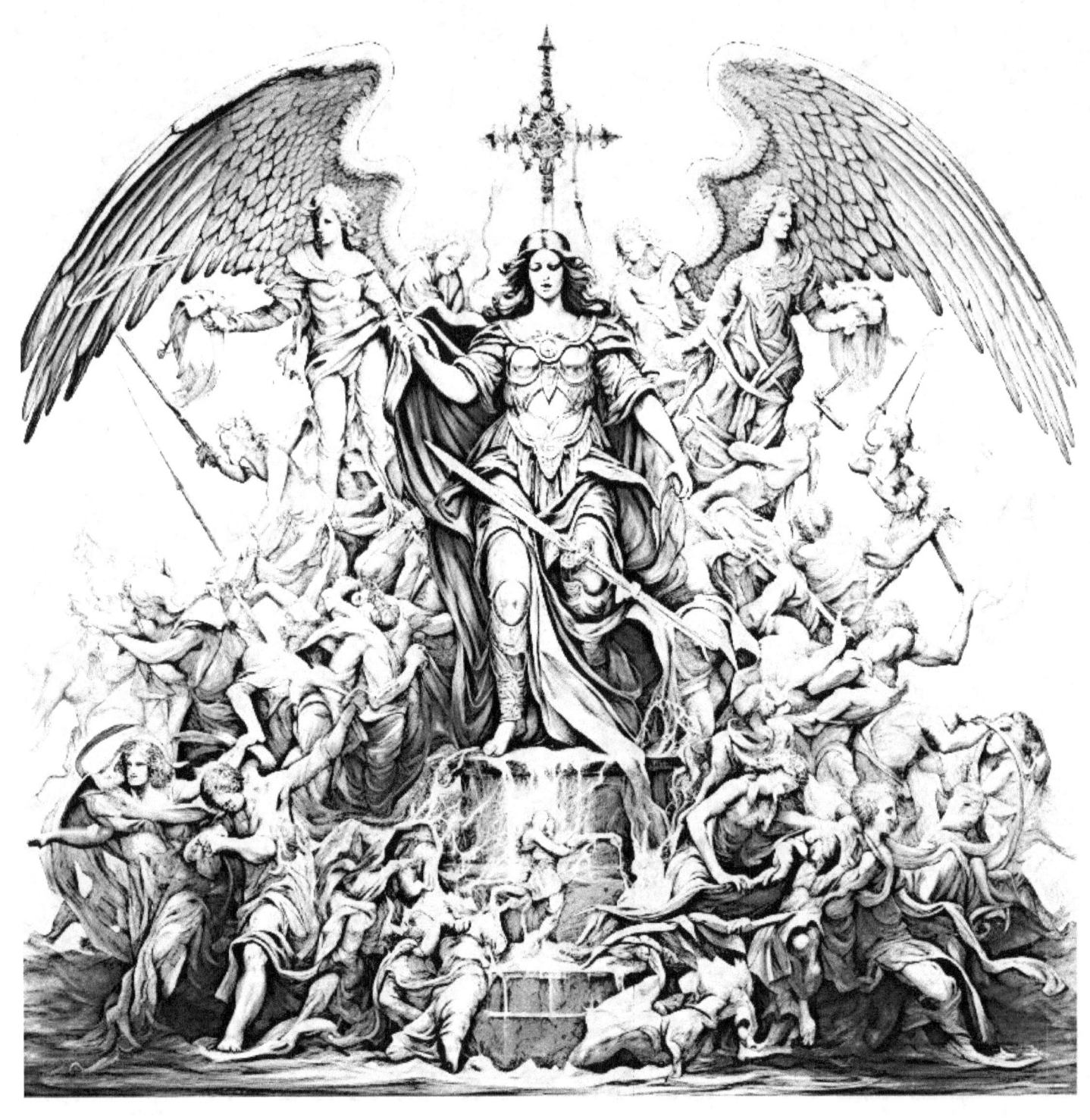

Jude 9

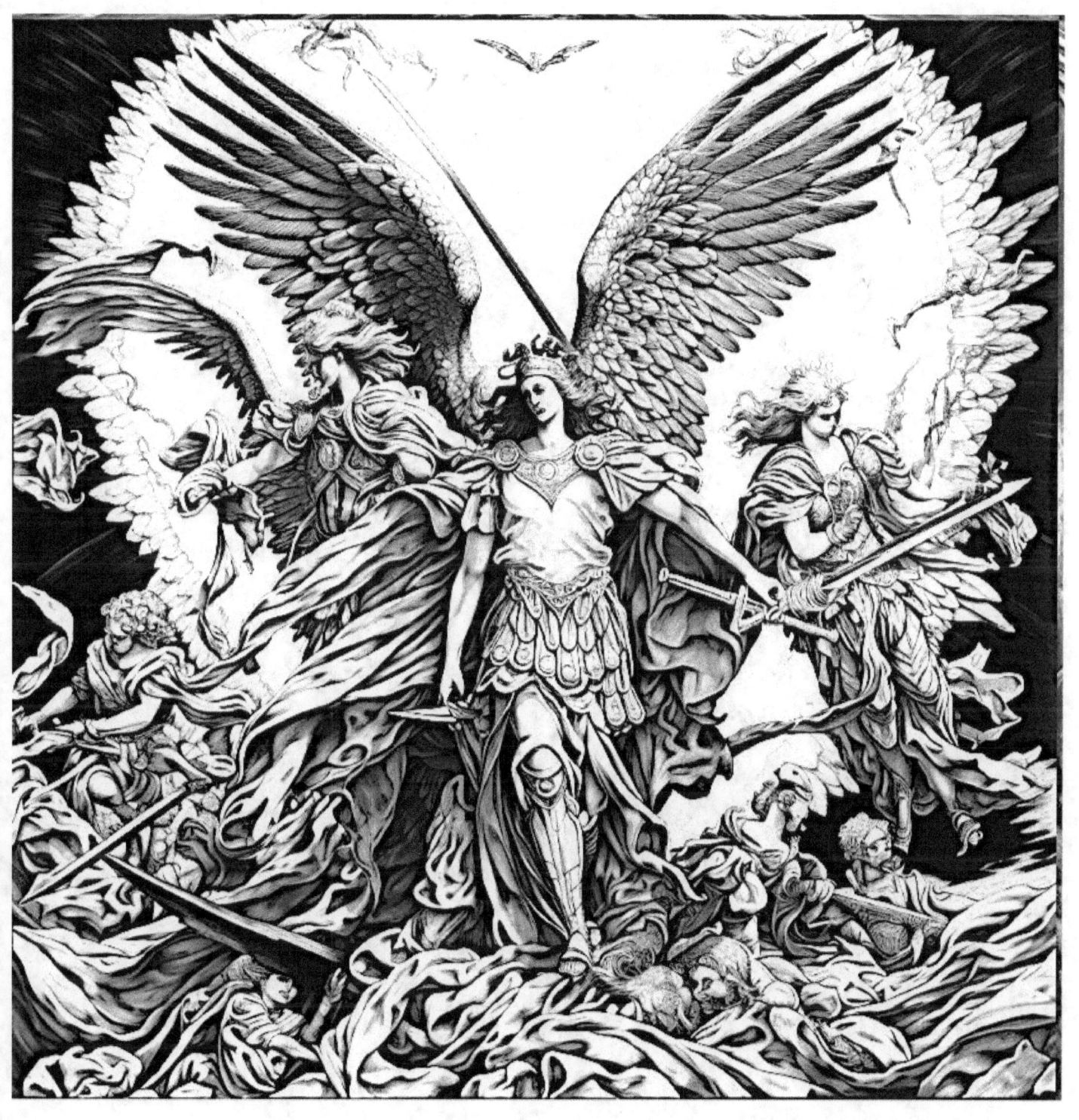

Revelation 12:7

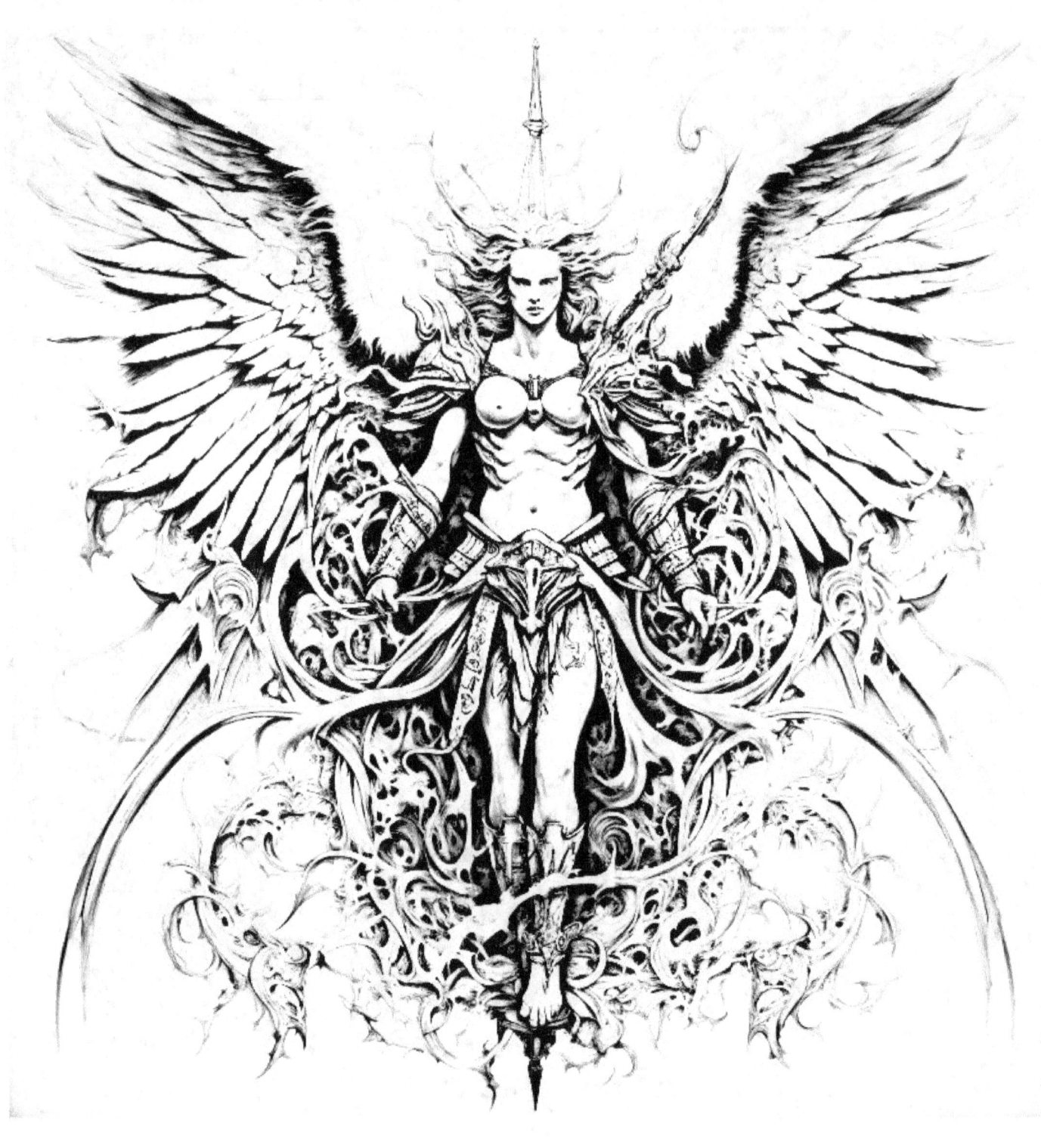

1 Chronicles 21:15

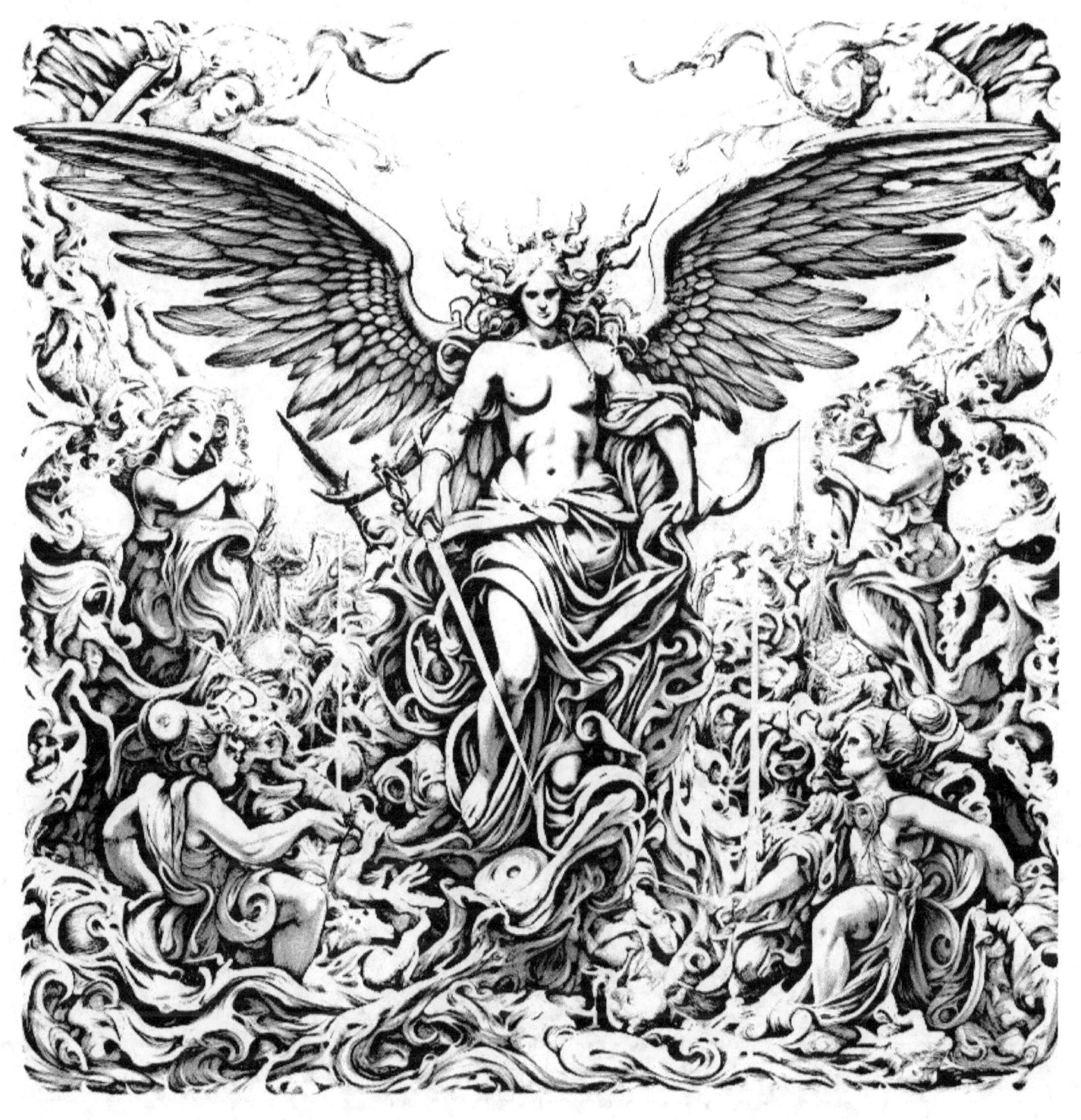

Luke 1:30-31

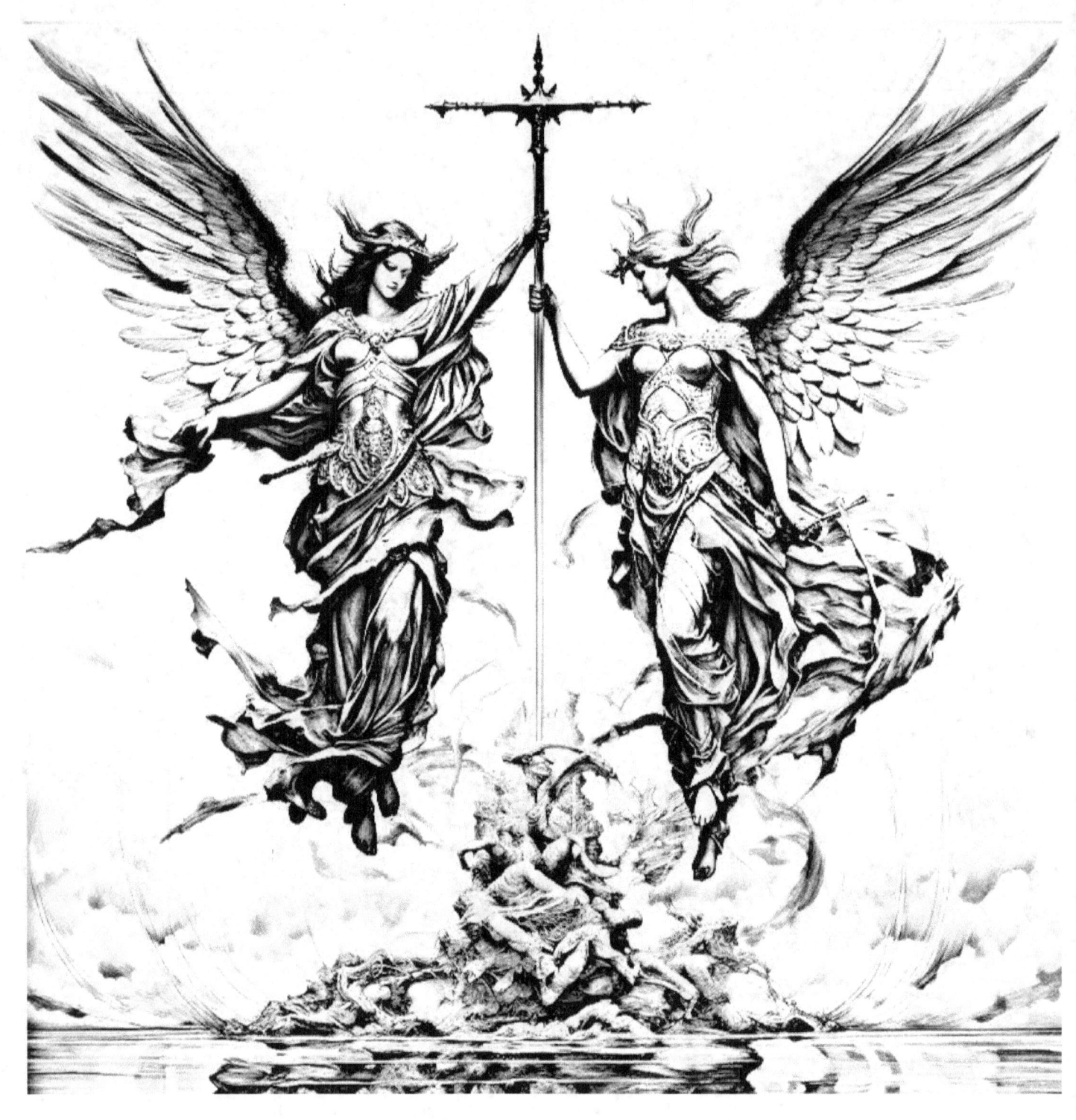

1 Timothy 5:21-22

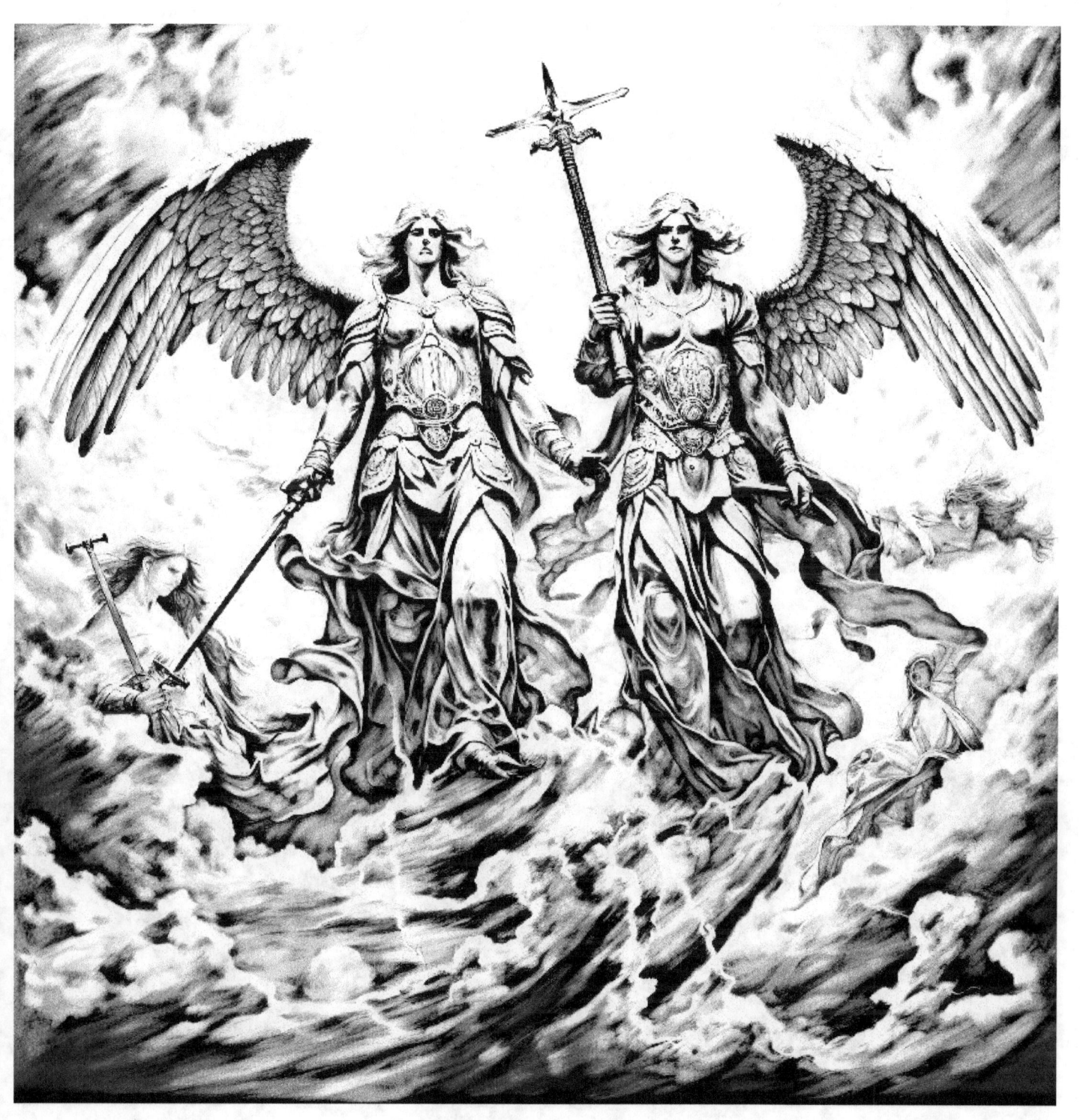

acts 12:23

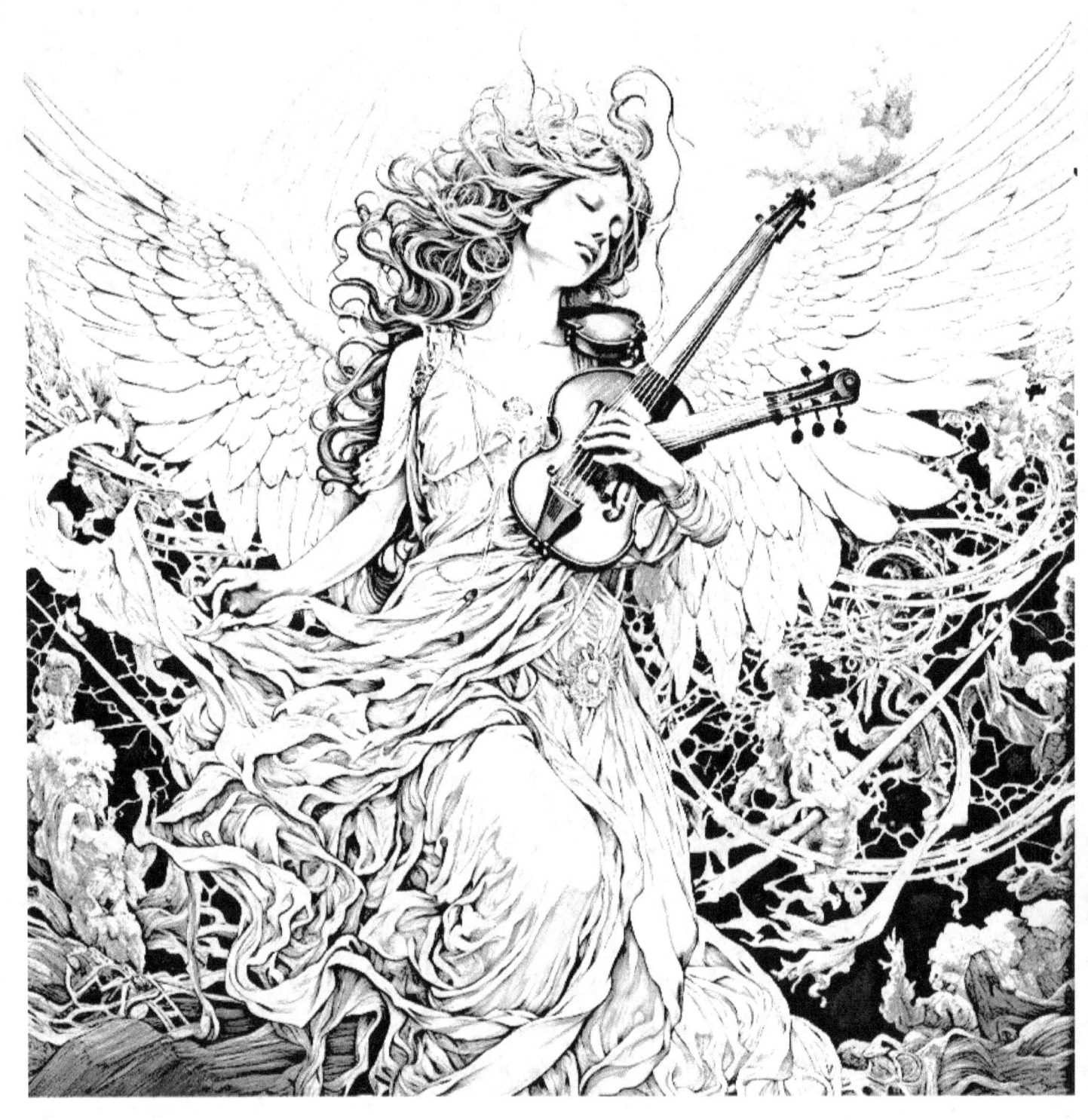

Luke 2:13-14

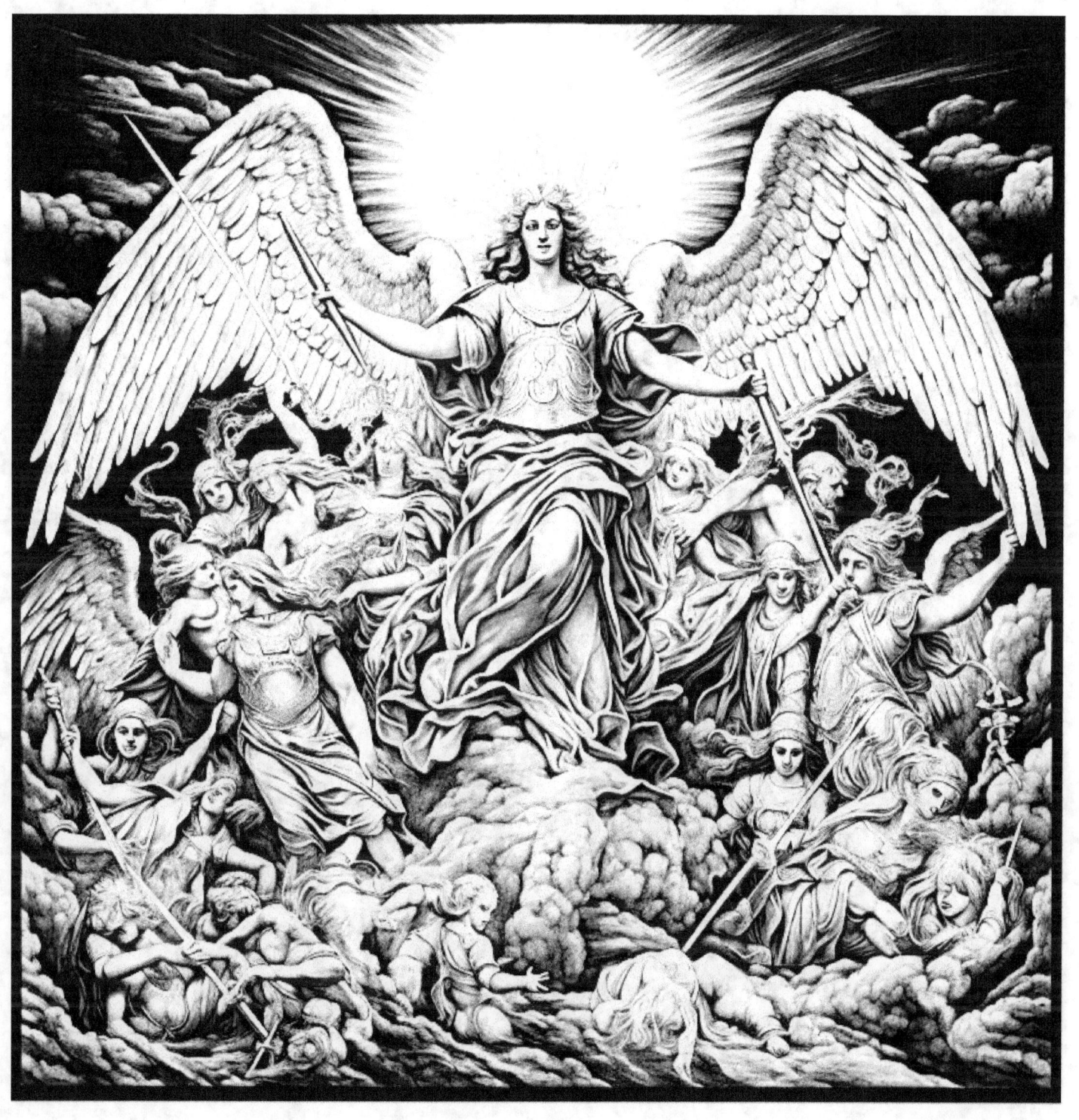

Revelation 3:5

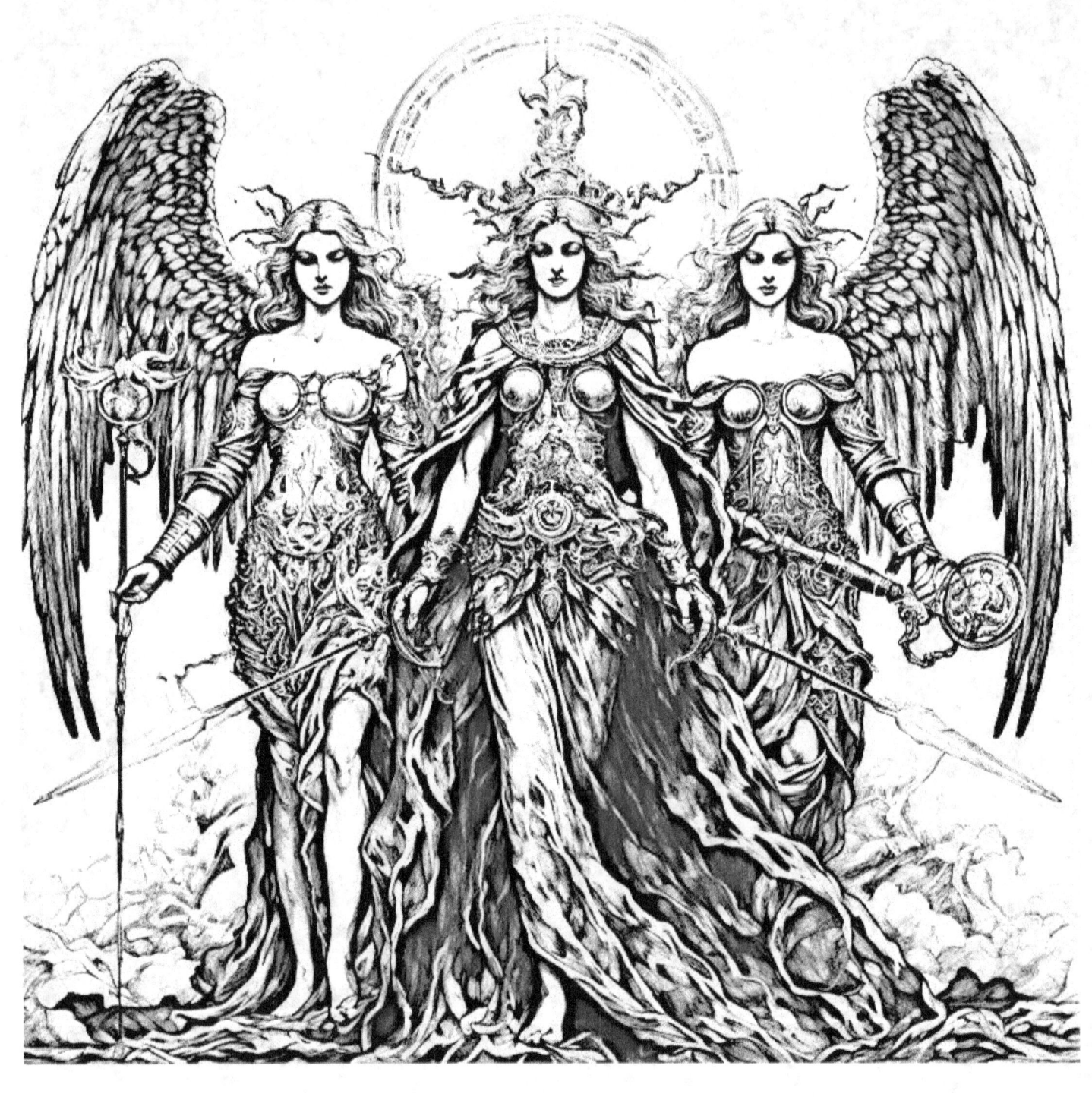

1 Corinthians 15:39-40

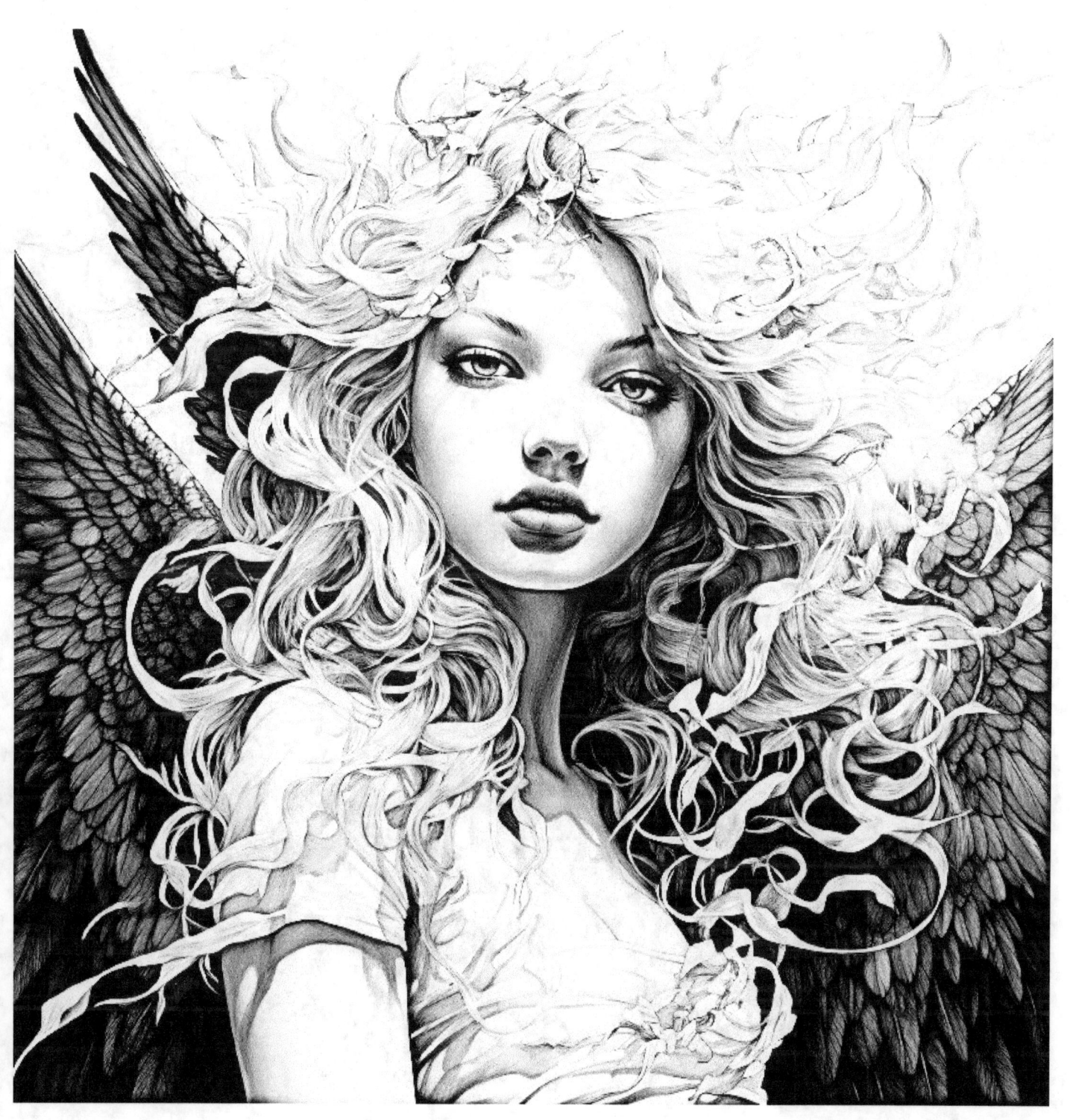

Matthew 2:19

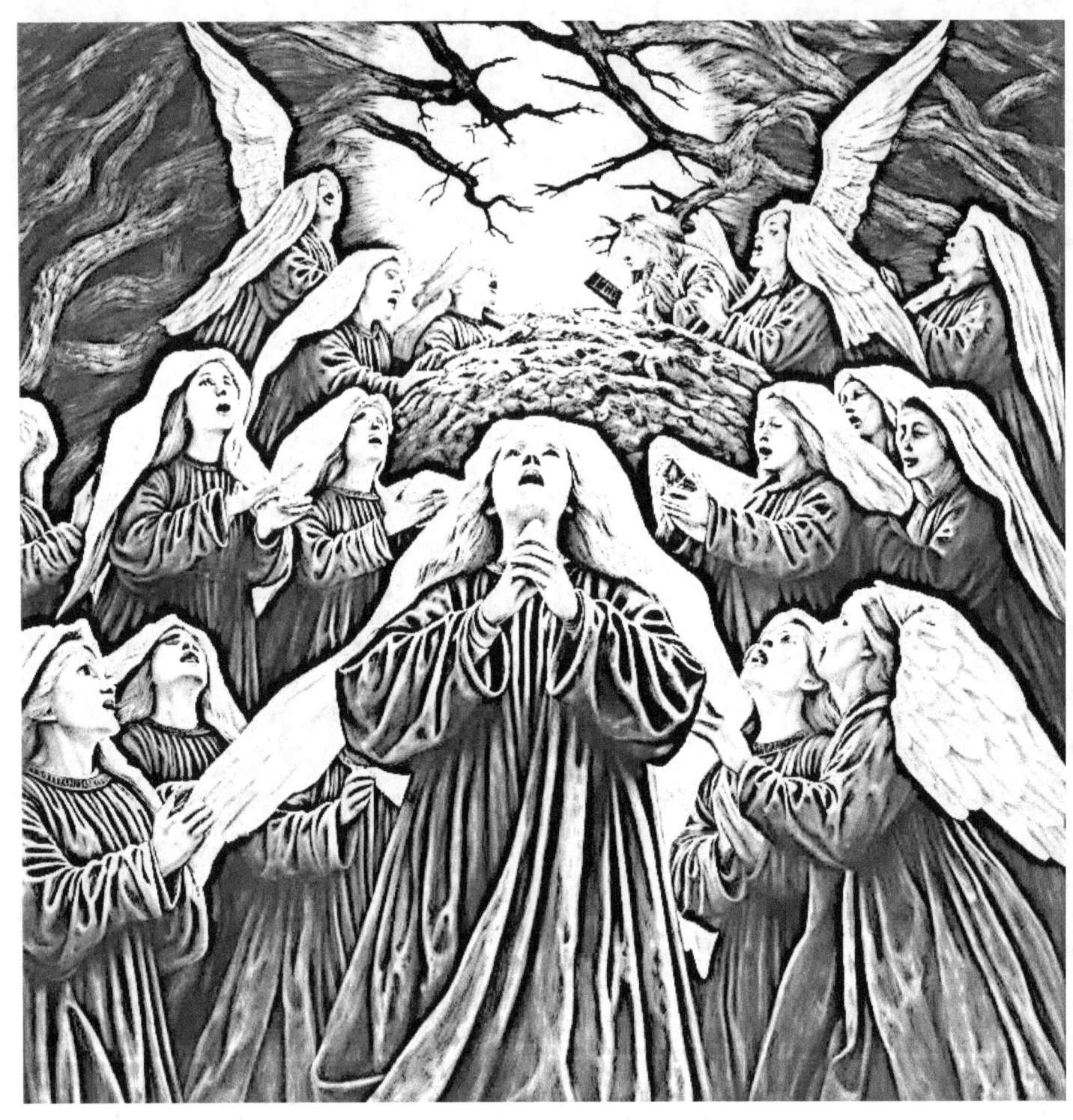

Revelation 4:8

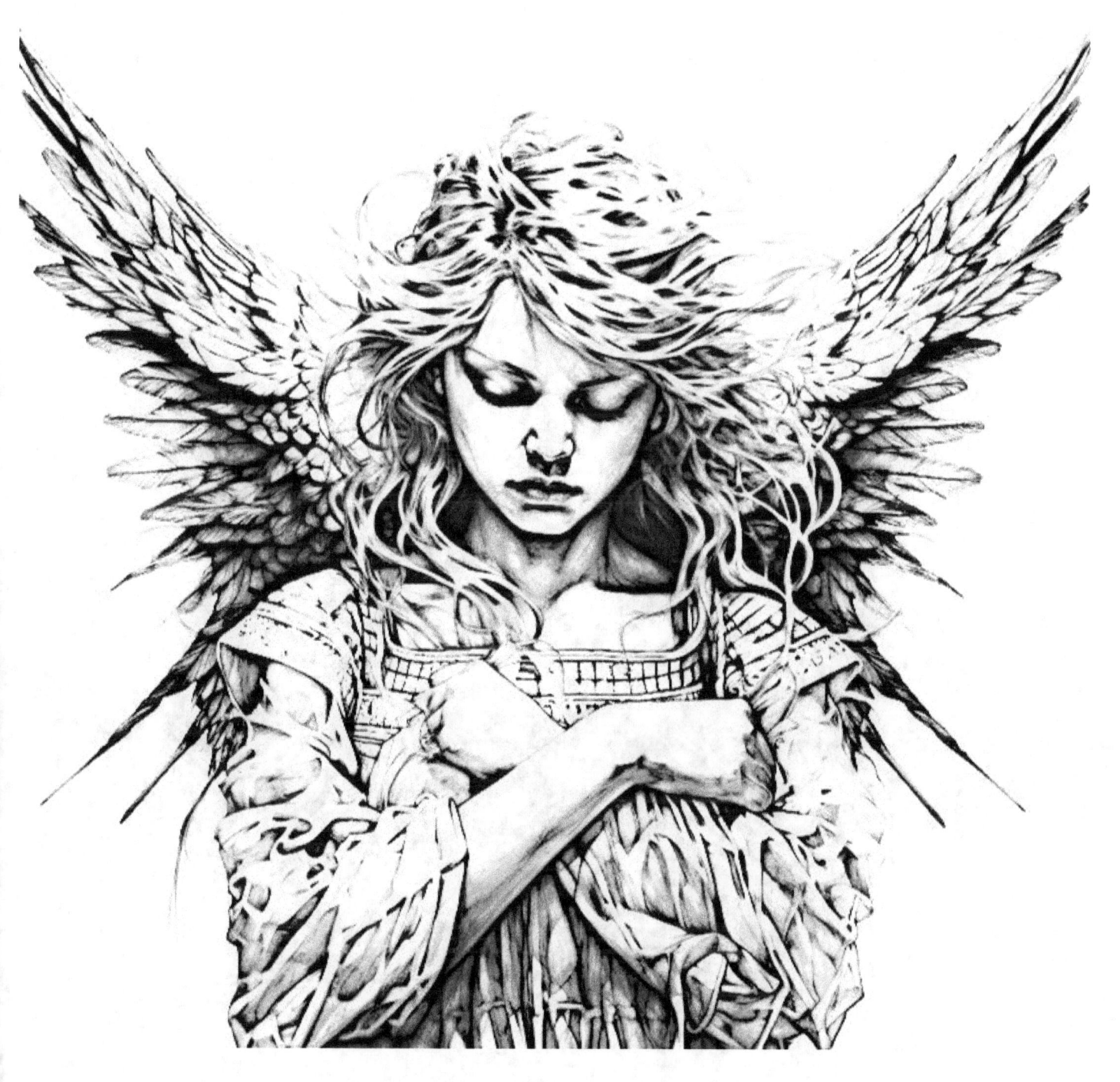

Job 4:15-19

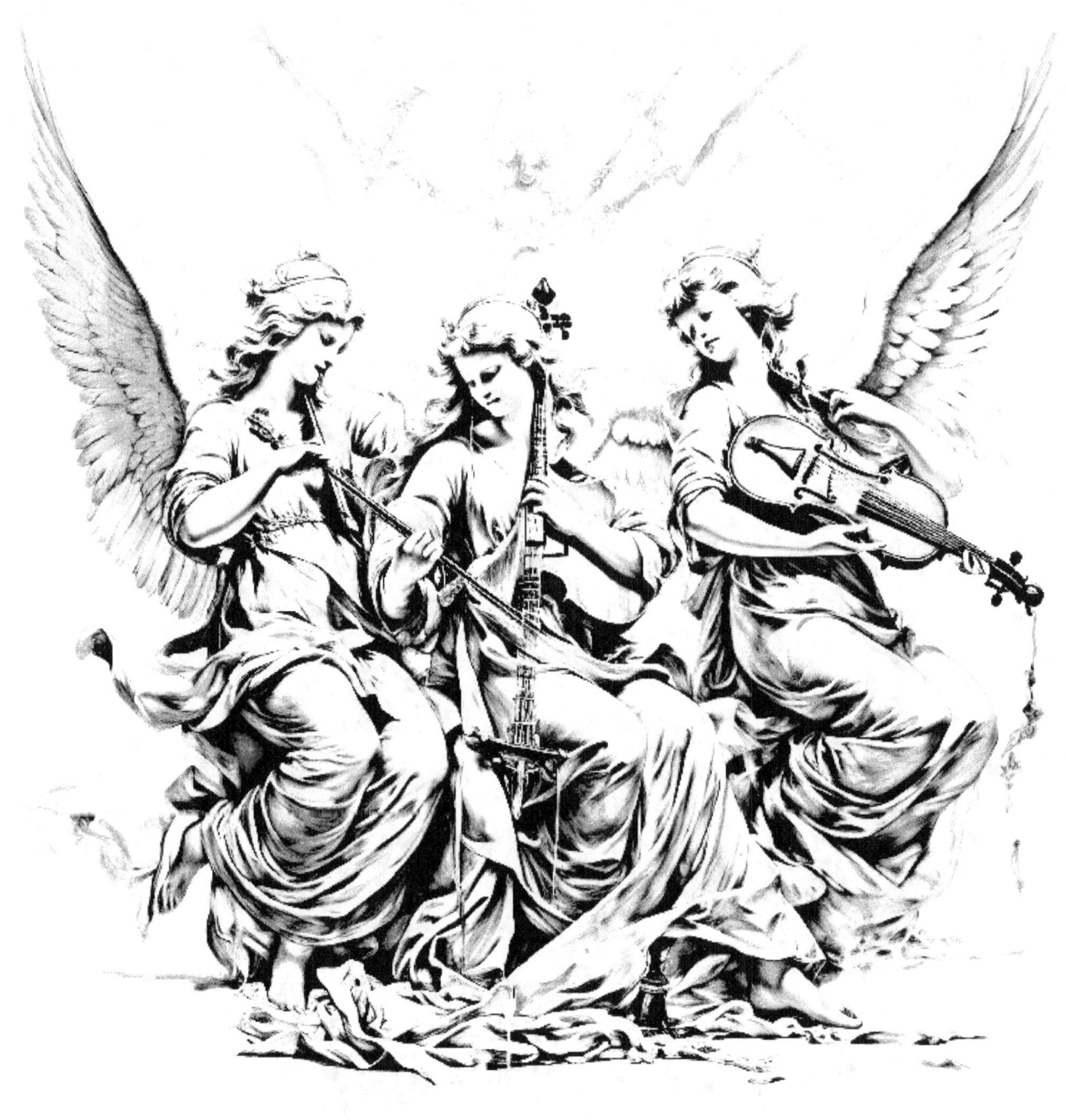

Psalm 103:20

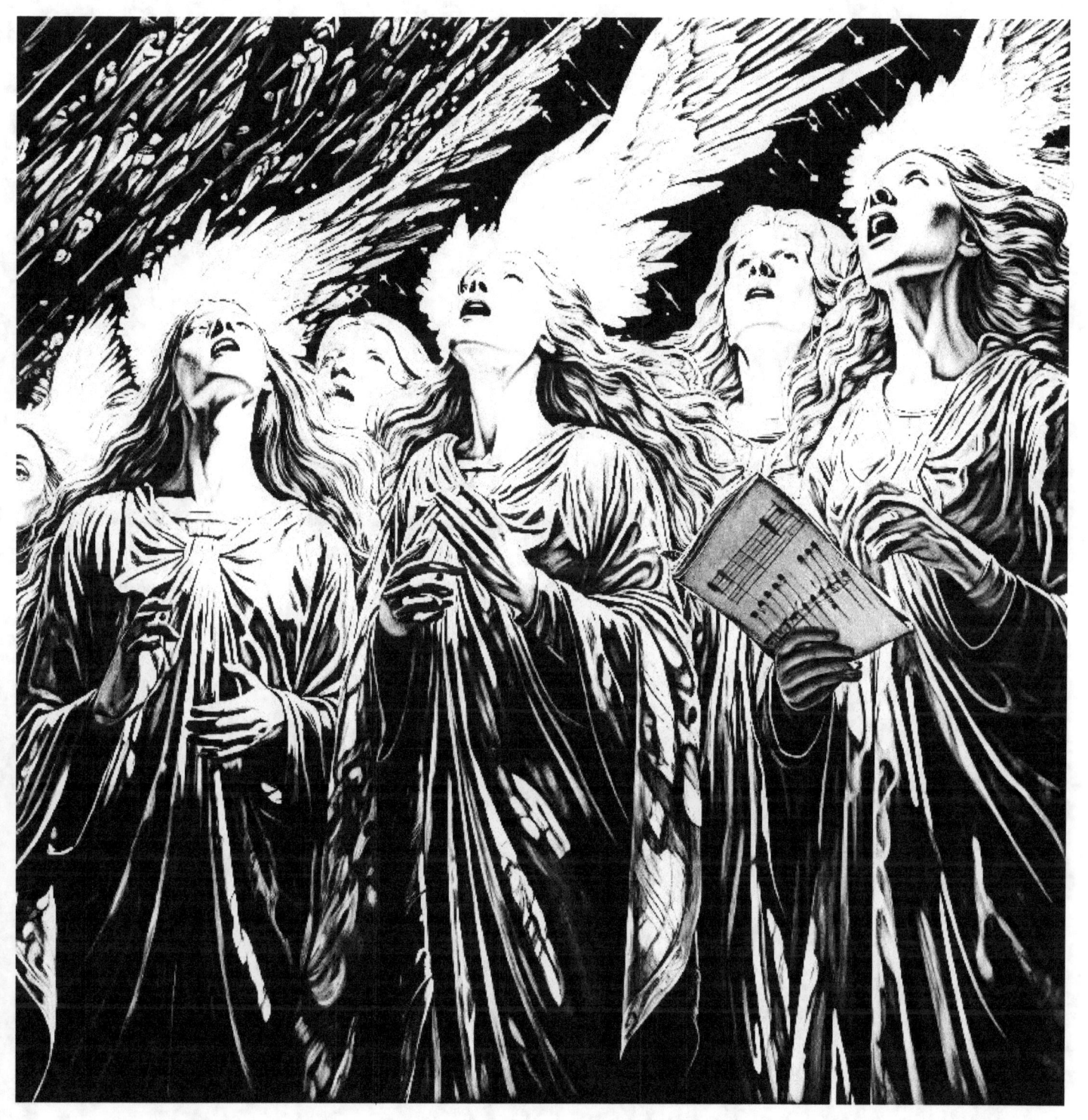

Psalm 103:20-21